SOUP

SOUP

foreword by eric schlosser

DK

London, New York, Melbourne,
Munich, and Delhi

Photography William Reavell

Editor Michael Fullalove
Designer John Round

Project Editor Robert Sharman
Designer Kathryn Wilding
Senior Jacket Creative Nicola Powling
Managing Editor Dawn Henderson
Managing Art Editor Christine Keilty
Production Editor Kelly Salih
Production Controller Alice Holloway
Creative Technical Support Sonia Charbonnier

Published in the United States by
DK Publishing
375 Hudson Street
New York, New York 10014

10 11 12 13 10 9 8 7 6 5 4 3 2

176114—11/2009

Published in Great Britain
by Dorling Kindersley Limited

A catalog record for this book is available
from the Library of Congress.

ISBN 978-0-7566-5697-3

DK books are available at special discounts when
purchased in bulk for sales promotions, premiums,
fund-raising, or educational use. For details,
contact: DK Publishing Special Markets,
375 Hudson Street, New York, New York 10014
or specialsales@dk.com

Colour reproduction by Colourscan, Singapore
Printed and bound in Singapore by Star Standard

**Discover more at
www.dk.com**

contents

foreword by **eric schlosser**

Some wonderful chefs have donated their favorite soup recipes to this cookbook for a simple reason. Proceeds from the book will support the work of the Soil Association, a nonprofit based in Bristol, England. Few Americans have heard of the Soil Association. But almost everyone has heard of organic food and sustainable agriculture, two of the causes that the Soil Association has been promoting for more than 60 years. Indeed, the modern organic movement was launched during the 1940s by a pair of British iconoclasts, Lady Eve Balfour and Sir Albert Howard. At a time when herbicides and pesticides and synthetic fertilizers were first being introduced on a wide scale, Balfour and Howard began to question whether these were good things. They rebelled against a mindset that viewed the land as just one more economic commodity, to be doused with chemicals for a short-term profit. They rebelled against a mentality that worshipped technology for its own sake, that eagerly sought to control and dominate nature. They embraced a much more holistic view of how we should treat livestock, the land, and the rural communities dependent upon farming.

The "Soil Association" seems like an odd name for an organization devoted to producing food that's healthy, nutritious, and environmentally sound. But the soil plays a central role in the thinking behind sustainable agriculture—both as a literal concern and as a metaphor for the interconnectedness of all things. What you put in the soil winds up in the crops that grow in the soil, winds up in the animals that eat those crops, winds up in the people who eat those animals. And every living thing, and every one of us, ultimately returns to the soil. You cannot mistreat one of these elements without harming the others. This is a deeply humble philosophy, founded upon a reverence for nature and a skepticism about some of mankind's latest inventions. It is a belief that we must try to work with nature, not seek to conquer nature. And it is the guiding spirit of many groups today, like the Soil Association, that are fighting against Global Warming, genetically modified food, and the toxic chemicals that are poisoning the earth.

We need to reduce the power of agribusiness and reclaim our government from the corrupt grip of special interests. But unlike many social movements, the battle for sustainable agriculture doesn't always have to be grim, hard work. As the great chef Alice Waters likes to say, this revolution tastes good. It's about shopping at farmers' markets or growing your own, eating food that's local and organic, educating yourself about the issues and learning how to cook. Every little bit helps. That's why a book like this can make a difference. Buy it, read it, use it often. I can't think of a better way to make friends and influence people.

Eric Schlosser
Author of Fast Food Nation

introduction

What does a book about soup have to do with the global food crisis and building a more sustainable and organic food and farming future?

Actually, everything! In preparing a simple bowl of soup for your family and loved ones sourced from fresh, organic, in season, and ideally local ingredients, you are taking powerful direct action to prepare the earth for a more resilient and sustainable future, both for yourself and for future generations. Whether your ingredients are coming freshly grown from your own backyard or you've bought them directly from a real person at the farmers' market, making the connection between the food you eat and the place it comes from is crucial to a healthy sense of cultural identity.

In a world where the problems we face seem so enormous and intractable, making the food connection is coined perfectly by poet and philosopher Wendell Berry when he wrote "Eating is an agricultural act." By eating food—in this case soup—with a good story, you are contributing to the solution at a local level, which, scaled up, has global implications.

This book has been planned with real food enthusiasts in mind. It is organized by produce, so you can look up whatever seasonal produce you've come across and find a range of different, wholesome recipes for it. The Soil Association, a UK-based organization that works internationally, has been working for over sixty years to promote a healthier food culture that puts the health and welfare of our environment, our farm animals, and people at center stage. We believe in the power of individual citizens to "be the change" and this soup book is a part of that revolution in our food culture.

Patrick Holden

Patrick Holden
Director of the Soil Association

techniques

The cornerstone of many soups is a well-made stock, and although the ingredients for it may seem humble and the preparation simple, the contribution it makes is vital.

making stock

The four stocks most commonly called for in soup-making are chicken stock, brown meat stock, fish stock, and vegetable stock. Made from bones and/or common vegetables and flavorings, they are easy to prepare and freeze well for up to three months. If produced from meat bones, stock is clear and relatively fat-free, although it will be gelatinous enough to set when cold. Vegetable stock is lighter and requires a careful balance of ingredients to make it flavorsome. Stocks should not be seasoned with salt—they are one of the building blocks for a soup, not a dish in their own right.

selection of stocks

brown meat stock is so called because it is produced from meat bones that have been "browned" by cooking in fat. It jellies when cold.

vegetable stock can be given extra depth by the addition of mushrooms, potatoes, and tomatoes that will offset the sweetness of the other veggies.

fish stock is quick to make, ideally from the bones and heads of salmon or mild-flavored white fish, especially flatfish like sole and plaice.

chicken stock serves as the base for many fine soups. Some raw or cooked chicken bones and a few standard aromatics are all that's required to produce a rich, gelatinous stock.

This recipe gives an ideal list of ingredients, but as long as you have the chicken carcass, onion, carrot, and one or two of the herbs, you can turn out a fine stock.

chicken stock

MAKES 1.5 QT (1.5 L)   **PREP** 5 MINS **COOK** 3 HRS   **FREEZE** 3 MONTHS

1 raw or cooked chicken carcass,
    roughly broken into pieces
1 onion, quartered
1 carrot, quartered
1 leek, quartered
1 celery rib, quartered

1 bay leaf
2 parsley stems
1 sprig of thyme
8 black peppercorns
1.7 quarts (1.7 liters) cold water

1 Put the chicken, vegetables, and all the seasonings into a large pan, cover with the water, and bring to a boil. Cover with a lid, lower the heat, and simmer for 2–3 hours, skimming off any foam from time to time.

2 Ladle the stock through a sieve into a bowl, pressing the ingredients well against the side of the sieve with the back of the ladle to extract as much liquid as possible.

3 If you're using the stock immediately, remove any globules of fat from the surface by skimming the top of the stock with a paper towel folded in two.

4 Otherwise, let the stock cool before chilling it in a covered container for up to 3 days. A layer of congealed fat will form on the surface. Scoop this off before use.

microwave chicken stock
If you are short on time, you can also make chicken stock in a microwave. Put the broken-up chicken carcass into a large microwaveable bowl along with the onion, carrot, leek, and celery. Add the bay leaf, parsley, thyme, and peppercorns, then cover with boiling water. Cover the bowl with plastic wrap (roll it back at one edge to allow the steam to escape) and microwave on high for 25 minutes. Let stand for 25 minutes longer, then strain.

For a rich meat-based stock, use either beef or lamb bones, but never a mixture of the two. If you have any bacon rinds or vegetable trimmings on hand, pop them in the pot too.

brown meat stock

🅞 **MAKES** 2.5 QT (2.5 L) • 🕐 **PREP** 10 MINS **COOK** 3½–4½ HRS • ❄ **FREEZE** 3 MONTHS

3lb (1.35kg) raw or cooked beef or lamb bones
2–3 onions, halved
2–3 carrots, halved

a bouquet garni (see p24)
2.5–3 quarts (2.5–3 liters) cold water
1 tsp black peppercorns

1 If you're using raw bones, roast them with the onions and carrots in an oven preheated to 400°F (200°C), turning them frequently, for 30 minutes or until browned. If you're using cooked bones, start the stock from step 2.

2 Put all the ingredients into a large pan, bring to a boil, then skim off any foam that rises to the surface with a slotted spoon. Lower the heat, cover with a lid, and simmer for 3–4 hours. Strain the stock through a sieve, pressing the ingredients against the sides of the sieve to extract all the liquid. Cool, then chill in a covered container for up to 3 days. Before use, remove any solidified fat from the surface, then bring the stock to a boil.

hale and hearty
A meaty stock based on beef or lamb makes a world of difference to hearty broth-based soups like French onion soup.

This is an excellent stock, with a good balance of flavors. The potato means it will not be clear, but since it is being used in a soup, that doesn't matter.

vegetable stock

◉ MAKES 1 QT (1 L)   **🕐 PREP** 5 MINS **COOK** 35 MINS   **❄ FREEZE** 3 MONTHS

1 leek, thickly sliced
1 large carrot, thickly sliced
2 celery ribs, thickly sliced
1 onion, coarsely chopped
2½oz (75g) button or cremini
    mushrooms, quartered

1 medium potato, thickly sliced
1 tomato, quartered
3 parsley stems
2 bay leaves
4 sprigs of thyme
1.5 quarts (1.5 liters) cold water

1 Put all the ingredients into a large pot. Bring to a boil, then lower the heat, cover with a lid, and simmer very gently for 30 minutes.

2 Strain the stock through a fine sieve, pressing the ingredients well against the sides of the sieve to extract all the liquid. Let cool completely, then chill in a covered container for up to 3 days before use.

light and fragrant
A flavorful vegetable stock
makes a good alternative to chicken
stock, whether you are vegetarian or not.

Ask the fishmonger for the bones when getting fish filleted, and check to see if they have any extra they can give you. Fish bones will freeze, well-wrapped, for up to two months.

fish stock

⊘ **MAKES** 1.5 QT (1.5 L)　　🕐 **PREP** 5 MINS **COOK** 30 MINS　　❄ **FREEZE** 2 MONTHS

1½–2¼lb (675g–1kg) salmon or white fish
　bones, heads, and skin (don't use those
　from dark, oily fish such as mackerel,
　herring, and sardines—they will give
　an unpleasant flavor)
6 black peppercorns
1 sprig of thyme

1 bay leaf
2 parsley stems
2 small carrots, coarsely chopped
1 onion, coarsely chopped
2 celery ribs, coarsely chopped
1 cup dry white wine
1.7 quarts (1.7 liters) cold water

1 Put the fish heads and bones into a large pan, breaking or cutting them up with a knife to fit. Add the black peppercorns, thyme, bay leaf, and parsley.

2 Add the vegetables to the pot with the wine. Place the pan over medium-high heat and let the wine bubble for 3 minutes. Add the water and bring to a boil.

3 Lower the heat and simmer, uncovered, for 20–25 minutes—but no longer, or the stock may begin to develop a bitter taste. Skim off any white foam from time to time with a slotted spoon.

4 Strain the stock through a fine sieve into a bowl, pressing the solids against the side of the sieve to extract all the liquid. Allow to cool completely, then chill in a covered container for up to 3 days.

5 The finished stock should be thin in texture, with a delicate flavor. It will make an excellent base for all kinds of fish soup.

Careful preparation of vegetables is essential—not only do properly cut vegetables contribute to the finished appearance of a soup, they cook more evenly too.

preparing vegetables

Vegetables are best prepared just before cooking: washed, peeled, and cut ahead of time, they are left exposed to air and moisture, which can lead them to deteriorate and lose their vitamins. Most often vegetables can be cut by hand, so a good sharp knife is vital. Use a large or small knife depending on the vegetable you're cutting. Here's how to prepare those most commonly used in soups.

chopping or crushing garlic

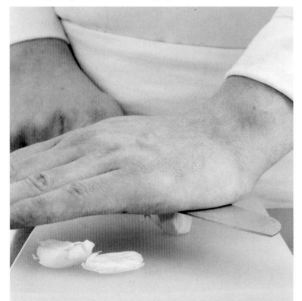 

1 Lay the clove of garlic on a cutting board with the blade of a large knife on top of it. Strike the blade with the heel of your hand to break the skin of the clove, but don't press down so hard that you smash the garlic.

2 Peel off the skin, then chop the ends off of the garlic. Chop the garlic coarsely, then sprinkle it with a little salt to keep it from sticking to the blade. You can then chop it finely or crush smooth with the flat blade.

chopping onions

1 Cut the onion in half lengthwise with a chef's knife. Peel away the skin, but leave the root intact—it will help keep the halves together as you chop.

2 With the onion flat side down on the cutting board, make two or three horizontal slices, cutting up to—but not through—the root.

3 Now, vertically slice the onion finely, being careful once again to cut up to but not through the root.

4 Turn the onion 90 degrees and slice across to make even-sized dice. Discard the root when you get to it.

peeling and seeding tomatoes

1 With a sharp knife, cut an "X" in the base of the tomato.

2 Immerse it in boiling water for 20 seconds, or until the skin begins to split.

3 Remove the tomato with a slotted spoon and plunge it into ice water to cool it.

4 When it's cool enough to handle, use a paring knife to peel off the skin.

5 Slice the tomato in half, then squeeze the seeds into a bowl and discard.

6 Slice the tomato half first into strips and then into dice.

cleaning and chopping leeks

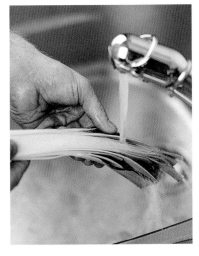

1 With a large knife, trim off the root and some of the dark green leaf at the top, then slice the leek lengthwise in two and fan it open.

2 Rinse the leek under cold running water to remove the soil that tends to collect between the layers, then pat it dry with paper towels.

3 Sit the halved leek on the cutting board and slice it into thick or thin strips, according to the recipe.

chopping carrots

Peel the carrot, then slice it lengthwise. Cut the lengths crosswise, then stack them and cut into batons. Slice across the batons to make even-sized dice.

sweating vegetables

Sweating chopped vegetables in oil or butter gives a soup a more pronounced flavor. Heat a little fat over low heat, stir in the vegetables, then add a pinch of salt, cover, and cook for 5–10 minutes or until soft but not brown.

Chopped herbs release more of their flavor than whole, but before the leaves of some herbs like rosemary can be chopped, they need to be stripped from their stalks.

preparing herbs

chopping herbs with tender stalks

1 To chop the leaves of herbs with tender stalks like basil, roll them together into a tight bunch.

2 Holding the bunch of leaves steady with one hand, slice across them with a chef's knife.

3 Using the knife in a rocking motion, chop the leaves finely, turning them 90 degrees halfway through.

using a mezzaluna

removing stalks

making a bouquet garni

A mezzaluna makes light work of chopping herbs. Rock it from side to side across them until they're chopped to your liking.

To strip the leaves off herbs with stalks, run the thumb and forefinger of one hand along the stalk.

For a classic soup flavoring, tie a sprig of thyme and parsley with a bay leaf. You could also include sage or rosemary.

Spices lend an extra dimension to many soups and, whether you're using them fresh or dried, they usually require a little straightforward preparation.

preparing spices

bruising whole spices

Before use, whole fresh spices like lemongrass are usually bruised with the blade of a heavy knife and your hand.

grating roots

Roots like ginger can be finely chopped by hand, but it's often easiest to grate them. Peel off the skin beforehand.

seeding chiles

Scraping out the seeds from chiles lessens their heat. Wear a pair of rubber or plastic gloves to do it.

frying in oil

When spices are cooked until lightly colored, their flavor gets trapped in the oil. Use the oil along with the spices.

dry-roasting

To dry-roast spices, place them in an oven preheated to 325°F (160°C), or cook them in a dry pan until lightly browned.

crushing

Dried or dry-roasted spices can be crushed by hand in a pestle and mortar or by machine in a spice mill.

Dried beans, peas, and lentils are perfect for soup-making. Little effort is required to prepare them—all you need to do is think ahead.

preparing legumes

The basic preparation of legumes is simple: first, you need to sort and rinse them; then (in nearly all cases) you need to soak them; finally, the legumes have to be cooked until tender. This can take anywhere from around half an hour to 3 hours. Once cooked, legumes are well-suited to puréeing, but they also work well left whole in soups.

sorting and rinsing

soaking

Whatever kind of legume you're using, start by sorting and rinsing them. Place the legumes in a colander and carefully pick out any husks or pieces of grit, then rinse the legumes well under cold running water.

Apart from lentils and split peas, all legumes need to be soaked for at least 8 hours, and preferably overnight. Place them in a bowl, add three times their volume of cold water, then cover and place in the refrigerator.

adding flavor

The flavor of legumes can be rather bland, so it's usually a good idea to add some aromatics. A bouquet garni (see p24) or a sprig of herbs will do the trick: bay leaves, parsley, rosemary, or thyme all work well. A pinch of cumin, cilantro, hot red pepper flakes, or caraway is another option, but you could also pop a carrot into the pan or an onion studded with cloves. Alternatively, you can cook legumes in a well-seasoned stock, but never season it with salt—it will prevent them from softening.

cooking legumes

Drain the soaked legumes, then place them in a large pan along with any seasonings. Pour in four times their volume of cold water and add 1 tbsp vegetable oil to keep them from sticking. Bring rapidly to a boil, and boil hard for 10 minutes, skimming away any foam with a slotted spoon. Lower the heat, partially cover with a lid, and simmer until tender. The cooking time will depend on the variety of legume (see right).

COOKING TIMES

Here are approximate cooking times for the legumes most commonly used in soups.

black beans	1 hour
black-eyed peas	1–1½ hours
borlotti beans	1–1½ hours
fava beans	1–1½ hours
cannellini beans	1–1½ hours
chickpeas	2–3 hours
navy beans	1½ hours
green beans	1–1½ hours
lentils (split)	25 minutes
lentils (whole)	45 minutes
pinto beans	1–1½ hours
red kidney beans	1–1½ hours
split peas	45 minutes

Among the easiest soups to prepare are those you process to a purée in a blender. The alternative is to use a food mill—this requires a little more effort, but the results are smoother.

puréeing

The secret to success with puréed soups is thorough cooking, so that the starchy ingredients that give the soup its body can be blended to a smooth purée. For that reason, always cook root vegetables and dried beans till they are extremely tender, but never overcook potatoes, or they will become glutinous and gluey. There is also a range of semi-puréed soups, in which some of the ingredients are blended to thicken the broth, while the rest are left whole for interest.

in a blender

1 Before blending, test the ingredients are really tender with a knife—they are only ready to purée when completely soft.

2 Blend the soup until you have a smooth consistency with no lumps. Do it in batches so you don't overload the machine.

3 The consistency of a puréed soup will vary according to the ingredients used and the way in which they're processed. But, in general, it should be totally smooth and lump-free. To remove all traces of skins, seeds, and fibers, you may need to push the purée through a fine sieve.

using a food mill

Working the ingredients through a food mill is particularly successful for soups that contain ingredients with skins and seeds, which blenders sometimes can't cope with.

semi-puréed soups

To thicken a soup but keep some texture for interest, purée about half of it and then return it to the pan. Gently reheat the soup before serving.

A little butter or cream stirred into a soup just before serving will enrich it (see pp32–33), but there will be times when you want to thicken a soup a bit more. Here's how to do it.

thickening

There are several quick and easy ways you can give body to a soup at the end of cooking. You could whisk egg yolk or a mixture of egg yolk and cream into the hot liquid. Another option is to use starch, in the form of rice flour, all-purpose flour, or cornstarch. Or you could make a paste from flour and butter and stir this into the soup before serving. But perhaps the oldest method of thickening a soup is with bread, either stirred into the broth at the last minute or incorporated into it earlier in the cooking process.

with starch

with flour and butter

Mix a little cornstarch, rice flour, or all-purpose flour to a thin paste with some cold water. Stir the mixture into the pot of hot soup, bring back to a boil, and simmer, stirring all the time, for 1–2 minutes until the soup thickens.

Combine two parts softened butter to one part flour. Gradually whisk small pieces of the paste into the hot soup at the end of cooking. Allow the flour to cook for 1–2 minutes, stirring all the time.

with egg

Added toward the end of cooking, egg yolk or a mixture of egg yolk and cream will thicken a hot soup and make it velvety. Remove the pan from the heat to incorporate the mixture, then reheat the soup gently, whisking until thick. Do not allow it to boil or it will curdle.

with bread

Bread has long been used to thicken country soups. For gazpacho (left), bread crumbs are blended into the soup at an early stage. But bread can also be added to a broth at the last minute, and stirred until it breaks up and thickens the soup.

Butter or cream stirred into a soup at the last minute will greatly improve its character, adding body and shine. For interest, you can flavor the butter and serve it at the table.

enriching

Both cream and butter make a quick and simple garnish for individual servings of soup (see pp36–39), but if you have another garnish in mind, you can add them to the soup to enrich it while it's still in the pan. Butters flavored with herbs, nuts, or smoked fish are another way of enriching a soup, although these are best served separately, to be added to the soup by your guests.

with cream

with butter

Add the cream at the end of cooking and, in a puréed soup, after blending. Stir it in well, then check the seasoning. If you've added a substantial amount of cream, you may want to reheat the soup gently before serving.

Cut 1 tbsp of chilled unsalted butter into cubes. Remove the pan from the heat and whisk it in a cube at a time—the soup should become glossy and smooth. Do not reheat the soup or the butter will separate.

with a flavored butter

Flavored butters are an ideal accompaniment to puréed soups and bisques. They are also easy to prepare and work well with a variety of ingredients. Blend the flavorings of your choice into the butter, then place the butter on a sheet of wax paper and roll it tightly into a cylindrical shape. Chill it in the refrigerator or freezer until you're ready to serve the soup, then simply slice it into rounds. You could also serve the butter at the table and allow your guests to help themselves. Here are recipes for two flavored butters that are great with a whole range of soups.

herb butter Mix 2oz (60g) softened butter with 6 blanched and finely chopped spinach leaves, 1 chopped shallot, 1 tsp each chopped parsley, chervil, and tarragon, and some salt and pepper. Roll in wax paper and chill until needed.

lemon and hot pepper butter Combine 2oz (60g) softened butter with 1 tsp finely grated lemon zest and ¼ tsp crushed hot red pepper flakes (or more if you like your food quite spicy). Season to taste with salt.

There's no need to worry if your soup hasn't turned out quite as you had intended—even the most accomplished cook occasionally produces a dish that's less than perfect.

rescuing

Whether you are unhappy with the finished consistency or think the soup is too highly seasoned, here are some quick fixes to set things right.

too thin

There are a number of ways you can thicken a soup that's too thin. You could whisk in a paste of butter and flour or a mixture of eggs and cream (as here). Or, you could add some starch in the form of rice flour, all-purpose flour, or cornstarch blended with water (for more details, turn to pp30–1). Another option is to stir in a few instant potato flakes or a little instant oat cereal.

too thick

Depending on the liquid you've used to produce the soup, thin it with a little stock, milk, or water. Once the soup has reached the desired consistency, taste it, season, and reheat gently.

stringy or lumpy

Even a soup you've processed in a blender can turn out lumpy or stringy. Ladle it into a fine sieve, then use the back of the ladle, a wooden spoon, or a pestle to push the ingredients through. Reheat gently before serving.

too salty

If you only ever add salt toward the end of cooking and use homemade stock that's unseasoned, the chances of your soup being too salty are slim. But, if it is, there are a couple of things you can do. Add a couple of raw potatoes cut in half and simmer the soup gently until they're cooked, then remove and discard them before serving. Alternatively, add a little sugar and, if the soup is also too thick, some cream, milk, or water.

From a single piece of seafood to a simple swirl of cream, a well-chosen garnish transforms a soup, adding extra color, as well as texture and flavor.

garnishing

For some soups, a garnish is an essential component—the sour cream stirred into Borscht, for instance, or the cheese-topped croûtes served with French onion soup. For others, a garnish is a way of introducing contrasting textures and flavors. Many ingredients can act as a garnish if they also complement the flavors of the soup, but here is a selection to suit almost every type.

with cream

Dolloped, swirled, or drizzled, cream makes an excellent garnish for thick puréed soups. Use heavy cream, whipped cream, sour cream, or crème fraîche. Yogurt is also a good alternative if you're counting calories.

with herbs

Fresh sage or parsley leaves fried in olive oil until crisp make a flavorful garnish for gutsy soups, but a sprinkling of chopped parsley, chervil, or cilantro instantly adds interest, fragrance, and color to almost any soup.

with shellfish
A whole shrimp, crab claw, grilled scallop, or (as here) an oyster poached and served in its shell makes a spectacular garnish for a seafood soup. A wild garlic flower provides the finishing touch for this dish.

with olive oil
As much a condiment as a garnish, a drizzle of fragrant, full-bodied extra virgin olive oil brings a Mediterranean flavor to soups, while looking appetizing and glossy on the surface.

with vegetables

Raw or cooked, vegetables make eye-catching and healthy garnishes. If small, like peas, they can be served whole. Otherwise, slice them into decorative strips, dice, or rings.

with bacon

Cooked until crisp and then crumbled, bacon makes a tasty garnish that looks attractive floating on the surface of a pale puréed soup. Here it is accompanied by pieces of pan-fried scallop.

with seeds or nuts

Toasted seeds or nuts not only look pretty, they also lend a satisfying crunch. Served with a vegetable soup, they are a good source of protein too.

with croûtons

Small dice of fried bread are a classic garnish. For about 40 croûtons, cut 4 slices of day-old white bread (crusts removed) into ½in (1cm) dice. Heat 2 tbsp olive oil and 2 tbsp unsalted butter in a large frying pan until hot, then cook the bread, stirring constantly, for 10 minutes or until golden. Drain on paper towels before serving. For extra flavor, stir in a finely chopped garlic clove a few minutes before the croûtons are through cooking.

with croûtes

Large croûtons are known as croûtes. To make them, cut a day-old baguette into ½in (1cm) slices, and toast until golden. Alternatively, place on a baking sheet and bake in an oven preheated to 350°F (180°C) for 15 minutes.

ways of serving croûtes

Croûtes are a versatile garnish. Rubbed with garlic, then topped with cheese and popped under the broiler, they are perfect for French onion soup (above). For fish soups, spread them thickly with a garlicky rouille sauce.

A well-stocked pantry will save you time and help you rustle up soups even on short notice. With the right ingredients, it will also be a source of inspiration.

pantry essentials

Putting together soups from the contents of your cupboards or pantry is a satisfying experience. Whether you're cooking for unannounced guests or whipping up a quick supper, with a few well-chosen basics on hand, you'll always have the ability to make a tasty soup. Here are the required items.

onions

basic vegetables

Onions, garlic, carrots, and leeks are the basis for countless soups, so it makes sense to have them available at all times. Obviously, they are perishable—store them in a cool, dark place.

frozen stock and bouillon cubes

A supply of homemade stock is a must. Make it in advance and store it in the freezer. For those days when you're in a real hurry, have some good-quality chicken, beef, or vegetable stock cubes on hand, too.

a selection of oils

From the best-quality olive oil for garnishing to the more work-a-day varieties such as sunflower oil used for cooking and frying, a good selection of oils is invaluable. The more unusual, like sesame oil, are available in small bottles—a blessing when space is at a premium.

garlic

flavorings

Salt and whole black peppercorns are indispensable in the kitchen, but there are other flavorings worth having in your kitchen cupboard, too. Wine vinegars, sherry vinegar, Worcestershire sauce, soy sauce, and fish sauce are frequently used in soups.

dried or canned legumes

Whether canned or dried, beans, peas, and lentils are among the staples of soup-making. Dried legumes do not keep indefinitely, so buy them from stores with a healthy turnover, and be sure to use them within a year—no amount of cooking will soften them after that. Canned legumes need almost nothing in the way of preparation—simply drain, rinse, then drain them again.

dried legumes

dried spices

You don't need a taste for particularly spicy food to make use of a wide range of spices—a pinch of hot red pepper flakes or a tablespoon of crushed coriander seeds may be all that's required to give a soup that extra dimension. Among the dried spices most often called for are cumin, coriander, caraway, nutmeg, fenugreek, star anise, cinnamon, and ginger.

herbs—fresh and dried

For the rounded flavor and complexity they give to soups, herbs are invaluable. The more popular, such as parsley and chives, are available fresh all year round, but it's handy to keep dried and frozen herbs on hand as well. They are generally more pungent than fresh, so use them sparingly. And keep an eye on expiration dates: frozen herbs will keep well for up to six months; dried for up to four. If you grow your own herbs, try drying or freezing them for use during the winter.

fresh herbs

canned ingredients

Canned tomatoes are excellent in soups, and in winter are likely to be more flavorful than fresh tomatoes. They even come already chopped. Make some shelf space for a can of tomato purée, too, and a can of sweet corn. Some coconut milk might also be handy.

dried pasta and noodles

Dried pasta and noodles are at the heart of many comforting soups, so it's worth making them a permanent feature in your cupboards. If space is an issue, a small supply of vermicelli, rice noodles, and udon noodles will serve you well.

dried pasta

However well we plan, we all have food left over at times. Cooked chicken and ham are obvious candidates for soup, but you can make good use of many other leftovers, too.

making use of leftovers

The ideal home for leftovers is in comforting rustic-style soups. Add the ingredient sparingly to begin with, then use your discrimination to decide on balance, texture, and seasoning. Recycling food calls for ingenuity and skill, so never give in to temptation and use your soup pot as a receptacle, or your soup-making skills will acquire a poor reputation. Here are some thrifty ideas for using leftovers.

stale bread

stale bread

Stale white bread is the perfect starting point for making croûtons and croûtes (see p39), which are a welcome addition to a wide range of soups. Processed in a blender or food processor to form bread crumbs, stale bread is also an essential ingredient in the chilled Spanish soup Gazpacho (see p107).

cooked meat

Cooked chicken, turkey, and game are all excellent in soups, as is cooked ham. Cured meats such as chorizo and salami work equally well. In general, leftovers of red meats are not suitable for making soup, although the bones from cooked beef or lamb can go straight into the cooking pot for stock.

egg yolks and whites

eggs yolks and egg whites

Making use of leftover egg yolks is never a problem. Whisk them into a hot soup toward the end of cooking—they will thicken it and give a velvety texture. Although less versatile, leftover egg whites are useful for clarifying consommé.

cooked vegetables

Cut into dice, shredded, or left whole if small like sweet corn and peas, cooked vegetables can be added to a soup just before serving and heated through. Alternatively, they can be popped in the blender along with the other ingredients and puréed.

leftover cabbage

homemade gravy

Capitalize on gravy's richness and depth of flavor by stirring it into meaty soups just before serving. If the sauce has acquired a skin since you first prepared it, carefully remove this beforehand with a slotted spoon.

boiled pasta

Small pasta shapes that have been cooked but not covered in sauce can turn a simple soup into a square meal. Add leftover pasta at the last minute and then heat it through gently.

chunks of cheese

scraps of cheese

Small chunks of Cheddar, Parmesan, and Gruyère never need go to waste when you make your own soups. Grate the cheese finely and use it to top croûtes. Broiled until golden brown and bubbling, these make a hearty topping for soups.

red or white wine

A small glass of white wine splashed into a fish soup will help bring out the flavor of the seafood, while a little red wine added to a rich meaty soup will lend body and depth.

cold potatoes

Cooked potatoes are a boon when making soups, since they give extra substance. Process them in the blender with the other ingredients or dice and add them to the pan just before serving and heat gently through.

leftover potatoes

recipe planners

vegetarian

mango and curry leaf soup
35 mins page 325

creamy pistachio soup
1 hr page 229

beet and apple soup
1 hr 20 mins page 78

jerusalem artichoke soup
50–60 mins page 164

creamy kidney bean soup
3 hrs 35 mins page 209

tuscan bean soup
1 hr 35 mins page 204

sweet corn chowder
40 mins page 96

chilled

tomato borscht

white gazpacho

watercress soup

mango, cilantro, and
pomegranate soup

rose hip soup

cherry soup

chilled melon and ginger soup

lettuce soup with peas

vichyssoise

hearty

porcini mushroom soup
🕐 35–45 mins (plus standing) **page 195**

white bean soup
🕐 2 hrs 30 mins **page 212**

minted pea and ham soup
🕐 35–40 mins **page 93**

mexican chili bean soup
🕐 50 mins **page 207**

creamy kidney bean soup
🕐 3 hrs 35 mins **page 209**

**cannellini bean and
carrot soup**
🕐 1 hr 10 mins **page 211**

**rosemary's bean soup with
italian cheese crisps**
🕐 25–30 mins (plus soaking) **page 214**

lentil soup
🕐 55 mins **page 217**

harissa and chickpea soup
🕐 1 hr 10 mins **page 221**

split pea and bacon soup
🕐 1 hr 40 mins **page 225**

soupe de poissons
🕐 1 hr 20 mins **page 239**

creamy smoked trout soup
🕐 25 mins **page 251**

italian wedding soup
🕐 1 hr 50 mins **page 314**

pichelsteiner
🕐 1 hr 30 mins **page 315**

tuscan bean soup
🕐 1 hr 35 mins **page 204**

healthy

carrot and orange soup
50 mins page 71

roasted red pepper soup
2 hrs 25 mins page 112

fava bean soup
1 hr 20 mins page 91

vegetable and chervil soup
30 mins page 66

widow's soup
45 mins page 67

beet and apple soup
1 hr 20 mins page 78

asparagus and morel soup
35 mins page 83

fennel and apple soup
40 mins page 84

edamame noodle soup
20 mins page 88

fava bean and mint soup
55 mins page 89

eggplant and red pepper soup
1 hr 5 mins page 100

classic tomato soup
1 hr 15 mins page 101

tomato borscht
50 mins page 104

roasted tomato soup
45 mins page 106

gazpacho
30 mins page 107

spinach and rosemary soup
40 mins page 122

allotment soup

spicy

pork vindaloo broth
🕐 3 hrs 35 mins (plus chilling) **page 312**

main meals

quick

chilled melon and ginger soup
15 mins page 320

pumpkin soup

watercress soup

white gazpacho

summer vegetables

This warming recipe is based on a French country soup and is delicious topped with a spoonful of pesto, some chopped fresh parsley or tarragon, or some grated Parmesan.

allotment soup

SERVES 6   **PREP** 20 MINS   **FREEZE** UP TO 3 MONTHS
COOK 1 HR 20 MINS   WITHOUT THE GREEN BEANS

3oz (85g) French beans
2 tbsp olive oil
1 medium leek, finely sliced
1 small turnip, cut into ½in (1cm) dice
2 medium carrots, cut into ½in (1cm) dice
1 large zucchini, cut into ½in (1cm) dice
1 celery rib, cut into ½in (1cm) dice
1 large potato, cut into ½in (1cm) dice

2 tomatoes, peeled and cut into
    ½in (1cm) dice
2 garlic cloves, finely chopped
2 quarts (2 liters) cold water
sea salt and freshly ground
    black pepper
6oz (175g) green beans, cut into
    ¾in (2cm) lengths

1 Put the French beans in a saucepan with plenty of cold unsalted water. Bring to a boil, cover with a lid, and boil for 15 minutes. Lower the heat, then simmer until tender and drain.

2 Meanwhile, heat the oil in a large saucepan, add the leek, turnip, carrots, zucchini, celery, potato, tomatoes, and garlic, and cook, stirring often, for 10–15 minutes or until they are soft but not brown. Add the water, season with salt and freshly ground black pepper, then bring to a boil, cover with a lid, and simmer for 45 minutes or until all the vegetables are tender.

3 Add the cooked French beans to the pan along with the green beans, and cook for 5 minutes or until tender. Divide the soup among six bowls and serve with some crusty bread.

A light, refreshing soup with a hint of spice, this is the perfect start to a summer meal. Try adding a swirl of cream or a spoonful of low-fat plain yogurt before serving.

carrot and orange soup

🅞 **SERVES** 4 🕐 **PREP** 10 MINS **COOK** 40 MINS ❄ **FREEZE** UP TO 3 MONTHS

2 tsp extra-virgin olive oil or sunflower oil
1 leek, sliced
1lb 2oz (500g) carrots, sliced
1 potato, about 4oz (115g), chopped
½ tsp ground coriander
pinch of ground cumin

1¼ cups orange juice
2 cups vegetable or chicken stock
1 bay leaf
salt and freshly ground black pepper
2 tbsp chopped cilantro, to garnish

1 Put the oil, leek, and carrots in a large saucepan and cook over low heat for 5 minutes, stirring frequently, or until the leek has softened. Add the potato, coriander, and cumin, then pour in the orange juice and stock. Add the bay leaf and stir occasionally.

2 Increase the heat, bring the soup to a boil, then lower the heat, cover, and simmer for 40 minutes, or until the vegetables are very tender.

3 Let the soup cool slightly, then transfer to a blender or food processor and process until smooth, working in batches if necessary.

4 Return to the saucepan and add a little extra stock or water if the soup is too thick. Bring back to a simmer, then transfer to heated serving bowls and sprinkle with chopped cilantro.

in praise of...
beets

The underrated and under-used, yet vastly versatile beet is good to eat all year round, as one of its many virtues is that it stores so well. A sweet-sour, ruby-colored soup is guaranteed to convert even the most beet-averse of diners.

This soup should be sharp, sweet, and spiced—the juice of a whole lemon, one or two tablespoons of sugar, and quite a generous seasoning of salt and pepper are recommended.

beet and apple soup

SERVES 6–8   **PREP** 20 MINS **COOK** 1 HR   **FREEZE** UP TO 3 MONTHS
WITHOUT THE HERB CREAM

1 onion, halved
2 garlic cloves
3 tbsp olive oil
salt and freshly ground black pepper
12oz (350g) raw beets, peeled and halved
1 potato, halved
4 eating apples, peeled and cored
1½ quarts (1½ liters) hot vegetable stock
  or chicken stock

1–2 tbsp brown sugar
juice of 1 lemon
2 tbsp finely chopped parsley, chives,
  dill, or cilantro, or a mixture
7oz (200g) crème fraîche, sour cream,
  or thick creamy yogurt

1 Briefly process the onion and garlic in a food processor. Heat the oil in a large pan over low heat, add the onion, garlic, and a pinch of salt, and cook gently, stirring once or twice, for 5 minutes or until soft. Meanwhile, process the beets, potato, and apples in the food processor.

2 Add the beets, potato, and apples to the pan and stew gently for 10 minutes, stirring occasionally. Pour in the stock, bring to a boil, then cover with a lid and simmer gently for 45 minutes or until the beets are cooked through.

3 Transfer the mixture to a blender and process until smooth. You may need to do this in batches. Season with the sugar, lemon juice, and some salt and freshly ground black pepper.

4 Stir the chopped herbs into the cream or yogurt, then ladle the soup into warm bowls and drop a big spoonful of green-speckled cream into the middle of the deep pink soup.

This rustic soup owes its substance to the beans. Buy fresh beans when they are available in early summer—they are quicker to cook and easier to digest.

pistou soup

SERVES 6–8   **PREP** 30 MINS **COOK** 1½ HOURS   ❄ **FREEZE** UP TO 3 MONTHS
WITHOUT THE PISTOU

for the pistou
3 garlic cloves, smashed and peeled
coarse sea salt, to taste
leaves from a large handful of fresh basil
2 small tomatoes, peeled, seeds removed and chopped (see p22)
freshly ground black pepper
1oz (25g) Parmesan cheese, grated
3 tbsp olive oil

1 ham hock, or a thick piece of smoked bacon, about 5½oz (150g)

7oz (200g) fresh white beans, such as cannellini, shelled
3½oz (100g) fresh red beans, such as borlotti, shelled
9oz (250g) flat green beans, sliced
2 medium floury potatoes, diced
3 tomatoes, peeled, seeds removed and chopped (see p22)
4 medium zucchini, chopped
salt and freshly ground black pepper
3½oz (100g) small macaroni noodles

1 To make the pistou, pound the garlic in a large mortar and pestle, then add a little salt and the basil and pound to a paste. Add the tomatoes and continue pounding and mixing until you have a thick sauce. Add pepper, the cheese, and the oil, mixing well, and adjust the seasoning.

2 For the soup, put 2 quarts (2 liters) cold water in a large stewing pot. Add the ham hock. Bring to a simmer, then partially cover and simmer gently for 30 minutes, skimming occasionally.

3 Meanwhile, put the white and red beans in a saucepan, cover with plenty of cold water, and bring to a boil. Simmer for 10 minutes, drain, and refresh. Add all the vegetables to the stewing pot. Season lightly. Return to a simmer, then partially cover and simmer for 1 hour, skimming occasionally.

4 Remove the ham hock and shred the meat. Remove half the ingredients out of the pan, mash with a fork, then return to the soup with the ham. Add the macaroni and cook until just tender. Stir in the pistou, and serve.

This soup is a perfect spring starter. Try serving it topped with a splash of extra virgin olive oil and cubes of bread fried in olive oil.

fava bean soup

SERVES 4–6   **PREP** 20 MINS **COOK** 1 HOUR   **FREEZE** UP TO 3 MONTHS
WITHOUT THE CROÛTONS

3 slices slightly stale bread, for croûtons
6 tbsp olive oil
3 large mild onions, sliced
1 leek, sliced
3lb 3oz (1.5kg) fava beans, shelled

4 garlic cloves, crushed
a small handful of fresh chives, chopped
4 new potatoes, peeled and chopped
salt and freshly ground black pepper
leaves from a bunch of fresh radishes

1 To make the croûtons, cut the bread into ½in (1.5cm) cubes. Heat 3 tbsp oil in a large frying pan over fairly high heat. Add the bread cubes and spread them out. Fry for a minute, then stir and turn them over. Fry for another minute. Spread the croûtons over a plate lined with paper towels. Pat with more paper towels to drain off excess oil. Set aside.

2 In a big stewing pot or flameproof casserole, heat the remaining oil over medium heat. Add the onions and leek. Soften for 10 minutes, stirring frequently.

3 Add the fava beans to the pot with the garlic, chives, and potatoes. Stir, then pour in about 3 quarts (3 liters) water. Season lightly with salt and pepper and stir in the radish leaves. Turn up the heat a little and bring to a boil, then let simmer gently for 15–20 minutes.

4 Let cool a little, then work through a food mill. Alternatively, process briefly in a blender, then press through a sieve. (If you prefer, you can omit the sieving, in which case the soup will serve 6–8 people.) Reheat until piping hot before serving, topped with the croûtons.

Quick to make, this soup transforms everyday ingredients into a splendid light lunch. Frozen peas, with their natural sweetness, make a good match for the fresh mint.

minted pea and ham soup

SERVES 4–6   **PREP** 15 MINS **COOK** 20–25 MINS   ✳ **FREEZE** UP TO 2 MONTHS
BEFORE CRÈME FRAÎCHE IS ADDED

2 shallots, finely chopped
2 tbsp butter
1 potato, peeled and chopped
1¼ cups hot vegetable stock
1lb (500g) frozen peas, defrosted

2 handfuls of fresh mint leaves, plus 2 tbsp
  extra for garnishing
5oz (150g) cooked ham, diced
salt and freshly ground black pepper
2–3 tbsp crème fraîche, to serve

1   Cook the shallots in the butter in a pot over low heat for 2–3 minutes until soft. Add the potato and continue cooking, covered, for another 7–10 minutes or until the potato is tender. Pour in the stock and simmer for 10–15 minutes.

2   In a separate pot, boil 1¾ cups water and cook the peas for 2–3 minutes. Add the mint leaves for the last 20 seconds of cooking. Put the peas and mint into a sieve placed over a bowl, reserving the cooking liquid in the bowl. Add the peas and mint to the stock and process the soup using a blender until smooth, pouring in enough cooking liquid from the peas to loosen the consistency. Stir in the diced ham.

3   For the garnish, stretch a sheet of plastic wrap tightly over a dinner plate. Brush with olive oil and press the extra mint leaves onto the surface. Cover with another layer of plastic wrap and cook in the microwave for 2 minutes, until crisp. Reheat the soup, seasoning with salt and pepper to taste. Serve with a dollop of crème fraîche in the center, garnished with the dried mint leaves.

If you have grown your own sweet corn, wait until the very last minute to harvest it—the quicker you get it from the plot to the pan, the sweeter it will be.

sweet corn chowder

⊘ **SERVES** 4–6   🕐 **PREP** 10 MINS **COOK** 30 MINS   ❄ **FREEZE** UP TO 1 MONTH
WITHOUT MILK OR CREAM CHEESE

4 fresh corn on the cob
2 cups water
sea salt
2 bay leaves
2 tbsp olive oil
1 large onion, chopped
4 fresh sage leaves, chopped,
   or ½ tsp dried sage, crushed
1 tsp fresh thyme leaves,
   or ½ tsp dried thyme

1 medium carrot, chopped
2 celery ribs, chopped
1 large potato, chopped
7oz (200g) cream cheese
½ cup milk
salt and freshly ground black pepper
half-and-half or heavy cream, to serve
dusting of paprika, to serve

1 Stand each corn cob upright in a large bowl, and strip the kernels by cutting downward with a sharp knife. Set the kernels aside. Place the cobs in a large saucepan and add the water, a generous dose of salt, and the bay leaves. Bring to a boil and simmer, covered, for 15 minutes. Remove and discard the cobs and bay leaves.

2 Heat the oil in a saucepan and cook the onions until translucent. Add the sage, thyme, carrot, celery, and potatoes. Cook for about 5 minutes, until softened. Add the corn cob stock and simmer until the potato softens. Meanwhile, place the corn kernels in a saucepan and barely cover with cold water. Bring to a boil and cook for 2 minutes. Set aside.

3 Add the cream cheese and milk to the soup mixture, then purée until smooth. Stir in the corn kernels with their cooking liquid. Give the chowder one more process if desired, to break up corn kernels slightly. Reheat, seasoning with salt and pepper to taste. Ladle into warm bowls. Drizzle with streaks of half-and-half and dust with paprika.

This extra-special version of the old standard uses fresh, sun-dried, and roasted tomatoes, and takes the humble tomato to new heights.

cream of tomato soup

SERVES 4–6 **PREP** 30 MINS **COOK** 40 MINS **FREEZE** UP TO 3 MONTHS
BEFORE CREAM IS ADDED

3½ tbsp butter
1 tbsp olive oil
2 onions, finely chopped
2 celery ribs, finely chopped
2 carrots, finely diced
2 garlic cloves, minced
12 plum tomatoes, about 2¼lb (1kg),
  quartered, roasted, and coarsely chopped

8 plum tomatoes, about 1¼–1½lb (600–720g),
  peeled and finely chopped
6 sun-dried tomatoes, finely chopped
1 quart (1 liter) hot vegetable stock
2–3 tbsp heavy cream
salt and freshly ground black pepper

1 Heat the butter and olive oil in a heavy saucepan over medium heat. Add the onions and sauté for 8–10 minutes, stirring frequently, until very soft but not colored. Next, add the celery and carrots, and continue cooking gently without burning for another 10 minutes, stirring from time to time. Add the garlic and sauté for another 2 minutes, stirring.

2 Mix together the roasted plum tomatoes, fresh tomatoes, and sun-dried tomatoes. Add them into the pan with any juices, and cook, stirring, for 5 minutes to allow the flavors to combine; if the sauce looks too thick or starts sticking to the bottom of the pan, add a little of the hot vegetable stock. Pour in the remaining vegetable stock and simmer the soup for 15–20 minutes.

3 Blend the soup to a smooth purée using a food processor or hand-held blender. Pass through a sieve or mouli into a clean pan, unless you prefer to make a peasant-style soup. Add the heavy cream a teaspoon at a time until you are happy with the taste and texture. Season with salt and pepper, reheat very gently if needed, and serve.

In Russia and the Ukraine, borscht often includes tomatoes as well as beets. This version may seem unusual, but you will love its rich color and fantastic taste.

tomato borscht

⊘ SERVES 4   **⏱ PREP** 25 MINS **COOK** 25 MINS   **❄ FREEZE** UP TO 3 MONTHS
                                                                      AT THE END OF STEP 2

2 tbsp olive oil
1 small onion, finely chopped
1 garlic clove, chopped
8oz (225g) raw beets, peeled
   and finely grated
1 tsp freshly ground toasted cumin seeds
¼ tsp ground cinnamon
8oz (225g) ripe fresh tomatoes, peeled
   and coarsely chopped
1 cup tomato juice

1 tbsp sun-dried tomatoes,
   very finely chopped
2½ cups vegetable stock
1 tbsp soy sauce
salt and freshly ground black pepper
toasted cumin seeds, to serve
sour cream or crème fraîche,
   to serve

1 Heat the oil in a heavy pan over low heat. Gently cook the onion and garlic for about 5 minutes, then add the beets. Cook gently for another 10 minutes, stirring from time to time, until softened but not browned.

2 Add the ground spices, tomatoes, tomato juice, and sun-dried tomatoes, then pour in the stock. Bring to a boil. Reduce the heat slightly, cover, and simmer very gently for 15 minutes or until all the vegetables are soft. Remove from the heat. Blend or process until velvety smooth.

3 Check the seasoning, adding the soy sauce, salt, and pepper to taste. Serve chilled, at room temperature, or slightly warm. If you do reheat the soup, do so gently over low heat. To serve, spoon into bowls, and garnish with toasted cumin seeds and a spoonful of sour cream or crème fraîche.

Make this soup toward the end of the summer when tomatoes and peppers are plentiful. It freezes well and will be a treat when defrosted for winter meals.

roasted red pepper, fennel, and tomato soup

SERVES 4–6   **PREP** 25 MINS **COOK** 2 HRS   **FREEZE** UP TO 2 MONTHS

1 large fennel bulb, peeled
1 red onion
2 red bell peppers, halved and seeded
1lb (500g) tomatoes
4 garlic cloves, in their skins
1½ tsp sugar
2 tbsp olive oil
1 large sprig of fresh rosemary, leaves only

1–2 tbsp vegetable oil
1½ tsp fennel seeds
½ tsp nigella seeds
14fl oz (400ml) passata
1 quart (1 liter) vegetable stock
1 red chile pepper, split and seeded
salt and freshly ground black pepper
handful of fennel leaves

1 Preheat the oven to 400°F (200°C). Cut the fennel and onion into wedges. Slice a cross into the base of each tomato and squeeze the juice and seeds into a bowl. Strain the juice and set aside.

2 Line a roasting pan with parchment paper and add the fennel, onion, peppers, tomatoes, and garlic cloves. Sprinkle over the sugar, drizzle with the olive oil, and scatter the rosemary on top. Roast the vegetables for 1 hour, or until the tomatoes are soft. Cool the vegetables before peeling the blackened skin from the peppers. Peel the garlic and discard the skins.

3 Heat the vegetable oil in a large pan and toss in the fennel and nigella seeds, swirling them around for a few seconds. Pour over the passata, the stock, and the reserved tomato juice, and bring to a boil. Add the roasted vegetables, pop the chile pepper into the pan, and season with salt and pepper to taste. Half cover with a lid and simmer for about 45 minutes.

4 Using a blender, process the soup until smooth and press through a sieve. Reheat, re-season, and finish with a sprinkling of fennel leaves.

This lovely, cool summer soup is just perfect when it's too hot to cook. If you can't find sorrel, try substituting spinach seasoned with lemon juice or zest.

avocado, cucumber, and sorrel soup

⊘ SERVES 4–6   **⏱ PREP** 5–10 MINS   **❄ FREEZE** NOT SUITABLE

1 ripe, buttery avocado, pitted and peeled
a generous handful of sorrel leaves (discard any tough stems)
¼ large cucumber, coarsely diced but not peeled

7oz (200g) Greek yogurt
1–2 cloves of garlic, peeled and chopped
salt and freshly ground black pepper
avocado oil, to serve

1 Place the avocado in a blender with the sorrel, cucumber, yogurt, garlic, salt and pepper. Add about ½ cup of water, and then process. As soon as it is smoothly blended, taste and adjust the seasoning, adding more sorrel if desired. Thin down with a little more water as needed.

2 Once you are happy with the taste and consistency, divide between 6 serving bowls or cups and drizzle a bit of avocado oil on the surface. Serve at once, or at least within the next hour while it is fresh and vivid.

PITTING AND PEELING AN AVOCADO

Slice the avocado in two, cutting all the way around, then separate the two halves by twisting gently.

Strike the pit with the blade of a large knife, then lift the knife to remove the pit.

Cut the avocado in half again and carefully remove the skin with a paring knife.

Make sure you add the greens at the last minute, otherwise they will overcook and the soup will lose its fresh taste and bright green color.

spinach and rosemary soup

SERVES 6   **PREP** 15 MINS **COOK** 25 MINS   **FREEZE** UP TO 3 MONTHS

3½ tbsp butter
4oz (115g) finely chopped onion
5½oz (150g) diced potato
salt and freshly ground black pepper
2 cups hot vegetable stock, chicken stock, or water
2 cups creamy milk (¼ cream and ¾ milk)

12oz (350g) spinach, stalks removed and chopped
1 tbsp chopped fresh rosemary
2 tbsp half-and-half, to garnish
sprig of rosemary or rosemary flowers, to garnish

1 Melt the butter in a heavy-bottomed saucepan. When it is starting to foam, add the onion and potato, and stir to coat well. Season with salt and freshly ground black pepper, then cover the pan with a lid and cook the vegetables over low heat for 10 minutes.

2 Add the stock and milk, bring to a boil, then simmer for 5 minutes or until the potato and onion are completely cooked. Add the spinach and boil the soup with the lid off for 2–3 minutes or until tender. Do not overcook. Add the chopped rosemary, then process the soup in a blender until smooth. You may need to do this in batches. Return to the pan and reheat gently.

3 Serve in warm bowls garnished with a swirl of half-and-half and a sprig of rosemary. If you have a rosemary bush in bloom, sprinkle a few flowers over the top for extra pizzazz. This is good with crusty bread.

Rich, slightly nutty avocado works well with arugula. Hass avocados are particularly good, but always buy extra in case one turns out to be blemished.

avocado and arugula soup

⊘ SERVES 4   **⏱ PREP** 15 MINS PLUS 1 HR CHILLING
COOK NONE   **❄ FREEZE** NOT SUITABLE

3 large (or 4 medium) ripe avocados
juice of 1 lemon
5½oz (150g) wild arugula
3¼ cups cold chicken
   or vegetable stock

¼ tsp harissa
salt and freshly ground black pepper

1 Peel the avocados and remove their pits, then chop the flesh and put it in a blender or food processor with the lemon juice. Coarsely chop the arugula (save a few sprigs to decorate) and add to the avocado mixture. Pour in the stock. Add the harissa and season with salt and pepper, then blend until smooth. Transfer to a bowl, cover and refrigerate for 1 hour.

2 Before serving, taste and adjust the seasoning. Pour into bowls or glasses, add an ice cube or two to each and decorate with sprigs of arugula. Serve chilled.

This verdant spinach soup is so simple; it takes no more than a few minutes to make, yet sings of the garden. It is beautiful served warm or at room temperature.

spinach and parmesan soup with crème fraîche

⦿ **SERVES** 4   🕐 **PREP** 10 MINS **COOK** 15–20 MINS   ❄ **FREEZE** UP TO 3 MONTHS
                                                                              BEFORE PARMESAN IS ADDED

10oz (300g) baby spinach leaves
2 tbsp unsalted butter
2 large shallots, finely sliced
1 garlic clove, finely chopped
sea salt and freshly ground black pepper

1 quart (1 liter) chicken stock
5 tbsp crème fraîche
3½oz (100g) Parmesan cheese, grated
grated lemon zest, to garnish

1 Wash the spinach thoroughly, drain, and shake until almost dry. Place a large pan over medium heat. Add the spinach, cover, and cook until it just wilts. Drain in a colander and set aside.

2 Rinse and dry the saucepan. Add the butter to the pan and melt over low heat, then add the shallots and sweat for five minutes, or until softened and translucent. Add the garlic and cook for 1–2 minutes, then season with a little salt and some pepper.

3 Add the cooked spinach and stir once or twice. Pour in the stock and turn up the heat. Bring to a simmer then immediately remove from the heat. Purée the soup in a blender until smooth. Return it to the saucepan and stir in the crème fraîche. Add the grated Parmesan cheese and check the seasoning. Then either reheat gently and serve warm, or allow to cool and enjoy at room temperature. Add a sprinkling of grated lemon zest before serving.

Here, the astringent bite of green chiles and ginger is tempered by the subtlety of herbs and delicate spinach leaves. Add a dollop of cream just before serving.

spicy spinach soup

⊙ **SERVES** 4   🕐 **PREP** 12 MINS PLUS 90 MINS MARINATING   ❄ **FREEZE** UP TO 2 MONTHS
COOK 40 MINS   BEFORE CUMIN SEEDS ARE ADDED

for the chicken
2 garlic cloves, finely chopped
1¼in (3cm) piece of ginger,
   finely chopped
¾ tsp garam masala
juice of 2 limes
3 tbsp Greek-style yogurt
salt to season
2 boneless chicken thighs, without skin
1 tsp vegetable oil

for the soup
3 tbsp vegetable oil

1 onion, finely chopped
2 green chiles, seeded and finely chopped
1 garlic clove, finely chopped
2 tbsp ground almonds
1 quart (1 liter) hot chicken stock
1¼in (3cm) piece of ginger, peeled
1lb (2oz 500g) baby spinach leaves
large handful cilantro
handful mint leaves
1 tsp sugar
salt and freshly ground black pepper
1 tsp roasted and ground cumin seeds,
   to garnish

1 Mix the garlic, ginger, and garam masala with the lime juice, yogurt, and salt. Add the chicken and coat. After 1–2 hours, heat the vegetable oil in a pan. Drain any excess yogurt off the chicken, drizzle with vegetable oil, and cook for 5–7 minutes on each side. Cool, then cut into small pieces. Pour any cooking juices over the chicken and set aside.

2 Heat the oil in a large saucepan over low heat. Add the onions, chiles, and garlic and cover. Cook for about 10 minutes, stirring occasionally. Add the ground almonds and cook for another minute, stirring. Add the chicken stock and ginger. Season well and simmer for 10 minutes.

3 Bring to a boil and add the spinach. When it wilts, add the herbs and sugar. Turn the heat off and remove the ginger. Blend until smooth. Pour the soup into a clean pan. Add the chicken and reheat gently. Check the seasoning and serve sprinkled with roasted ground cumin seeds.

in praise of...
lettuce

If you grow your own vegetables, it is easy to end up with an abundance of lettuces, and soup is a great way to use them for something delicious and different.

Don't used lettuces that have bolted for this—they will have bitter cores. Some of the leaves may still be good to use, though. Taste before using.

lettuce soup with peas

⊘ **SERVES** 4   🕑 **PREP** 30 MINS, PLUS 30 MINS CHILLING   ❄ **FREEZE** NOT SUITABLE

4½oz (125g) peas (shelled weight)
1 small garlic clove
pinch of coarse salt
2 medium heads lettuce (about 1lb 2oz/
   500g in total), cleaned, torn into
   pieces, and solid cores discarded

1 cup plain yogurt
¾in (2cm) piece fresh ginger, peeled
   and finely grated
handful of mint leaves
juice of ½ lemon
salt and freshly ground black pepper

1 Bring a small amount of water to a boil in a pan, add the peas, and cook for 1 minute. Drain (reserving the cooking water), cool under cold running water, and refrigerate. Cut the garlic in half, remove any green at the center, and discard. Crush the halves along with a pinch of coarse salt.

2 Combine the garlic with all the other ingredients (except the peas) in a food processor or blender, adding just enough of the reserved cooking water to get the blades moving or until the desired consistency is achieved—this will vary according to the type of lettuce and the kind of machine you are using, but it is nice if you can get it fairly smooth, with a bit of texture.

3 Transfer the soup to a large bowl and chill for 30 minutes. When ready to serve, stir through the cooked peas, leaving a few to garnish.

CHOOSING AND PREPARING LETTUCE
Search your farmers' market for lettuces with fresh-looking leaves and a silky, slightly firm heart. Avoid any that are wilted or bruised. To clean, pat the leaves with damp paper towels, then tear them—rather than cut—to size.

Serve this velvety smooth soup hot, topped with shavings of Parmesan cheese, or chilled with an extra swirl of cream or crème fraîche.

watercress soup

⊘ **SERVES** 4   🕐 **PREP** 10 MINS **COOK** 15 MINS   ❄ **FREEZE** 3 MONTHS

2 tbsp butter
1 onion, finely chopped
6oz (175g) watercress
3 ripe pears, cored and coarsely chopped
1 quart (1 liter) vegetable stock

salt and freshly ground black pepper
¾ cup heavy cream
juice of ½ lemon
Parmesan cheese, shaved, to serve
olive oil, to drizzle

1 Melt the butter in a saucepan and cook the onion for 10 minutes, or until soft, stirring occasionally to prevent burning. Meanwhile, trim the watercress and pick off the leaves. Add the watercress stalks to the onion with the pears and stock, and season with salt and pepper.

2 Bring to a boil, cover, and simmer gently for 15 minutes. Remove from the heat and pour into a blender along with the watercress leaves. Process until the soup has a very smooth texture.

3 Stir in the cream and lemon juice, adjust the seasoning, and serve sprinkled with Parmesan shavings and drizzled with a little oil. The soup can be made up to 4 hours in advance and refrigerated until ready to use. To serve chilled, pour the soup into chilled bowls, top with crushed ice, and drizzle with a little olive oil.

CHOOSING WATERCRESS
Locally produced watercress with fresh, round leaves and thick stalks are best. Unwashed leaves will keep in the fridge for several days, but ready-washed ones must be eaten quickly.

winter vegetables

Simple, affordable, and immensely satisfying, this hearty soup makes a warming meal when accompanied with some freshly baked crusty bread.

cream of vegetable soup

SERVES 6   **PREP** 15 MINS **COOK** 40–55 MINS   **FREEZE** UP TO 3 MONTHS
WITHOUT HALF-AND-HALF OR MILK

3 tbsp butter
2 carrots, sliced
1 leek (white part only), sliced
2 parsnips, sliced
1 onion, sliced
1 small turnip, sliced
3 celery ribs, sliced
1 potato, sliced

5 cups hot vegetable stock
2 tsp fresh thyme leaves
1 bay leaf
pinch of grated nutmeg
salt and freshly ground black pepper
3 tbsp half-and-half
3 tbsp milk
bunch of chives, snipped, to garnish

1 Melt the butter in a large pan, add the carrots, leek, parsnips, onion, turnip, celery, and potato, and stir to coat well. Cover the pan with a lid and cook for 10–15 minutes or until the vegetables have softened.

2 Add the stock, thyme, bay leaf, and nutmeg, then season with salt and freshly ground black pepper. Bring to a boil and simmer, uncovered, for 30–40 minutes or until the vegetables are meltingly soft. Scoop out the bay leaf and discard.

3 Process the soup in a blender until smooth. You may need to do this in batches. If you like the texture of your soups very smooth, strain it through a fine sieve; otherwise, leave it as it is. Stir in the half-and-half and milk, adding more milk if the consistency is still too thick. Season with salt and freshly ground black pepper, then reheat gently. Garnish with the chives and serve immediately.

This is a substantial soup that is a meal in itself. Mix and match whatever vegetables are in season—zucchini, cabbage, and leeks are all excellent in a minestrone.

minestrone soup

⊘ SERVES 4–6   **🕐 PREP** 20 MINS, PLUS 8 HOURS SOAKING **❄ FREEZE** UP TO 1 MONTH
COOK 1¾ HRS   AT THE END OF STEP 2

3½oz (100g) dried white cannellini beans
2 tbsp olive oil
2 celery ribs, finely chopped
2 carrots, finely chopped
1 onion, finely chopped
1 x 14½oz (400g) can chopped tomatoes

2½ cups hot vegetable stock
  or chicken stock
salt and freshly ground black pepper
2oz (60g) small short-cut pasta
4 tbsp chopped flat-leaf parsley
1½oz (40g) Parmesan, finely grated

1 Put the dried beans in a large bowl, cover with cold water, and leave to soak in the fridge for at least 8 hours or overnight. Drain the beans, then place them in a large saucepan and cover with cold water. Bring to a boil, then boil hard for 10 minutes, skimming the surface of any foam with a slotted spoon. Lower the heat, partially cover the pan, and simmer for 1 hour or until the beans are tender. Drain and set aside.

2 Heat the oil in the rinsed-out pan over medium heat. Add the celery, carrots, and onion, and cook, stirring occasionally, for 5 minutes or until tender. Stir in the cooked beans, then add the tomatoes and their juice, the stock, and some salt and freshly ground black pepper. Bring to a boil, stirring all the time, then cover with a lid and simmer for 20 minutes.

3 Add the pasta and simmer for 10–15 minutes or until it is cooked but still firm to the bite. Stir in the parsley and half the Parmesan, then adjust the seasoning. Serve hot, sprinkled with the remaining Parmesan.

Mounded together in the center of the bowl, the vegetables in this soup resemble coins—which is one of the reasons it got its name. The other is that it is very inexpensive to make.

"penny" soup

⊘ SERVES 4   **◕ PREP** 15 MINS **COOK** 30 MINS   **❄ FREEZE** UP TO 3 MONTHS
WITH ALL VEGETABLES BLENDED

1 leek, rinsed well
11oz (300g) potatoes
9oz (250g) large carrots
6oz (175g) small sweet potatoes
1 tbsp olive oil

1 tbsp butter
2 cups hot vegetable stock
1 tbsp chopped flat-leaf parsley
salt and freshly ground black pepper

1 Slice the vegetables into ⅛in (3mm) rounds. Heat the oil and butter in a large saucepan, add the leeks, and cook over medium heat, stirring frequently, for 3–4 minutes or until soft. Add the potatoes, carrots, and sweet potatoes and cook, stirring, for 1 minute.

2 Pour in the stock, then bring to a boil, cover with a lid, and simmer for 20 minutes or until the vegetables are tender but not soft. Transfer about one-third of the vegetables to a blender or food processor with a little of the liquid and blend to a smooth purée, then return to the pan. Stir in the parsley, season to taste with salt and freshly ground black pepper, and serve, with the vegetables in a little mound in the center.

Leftovers of this big warming soup from Tuscany are never thrown away, but used to make the sturdy Ribollita (see right). Both are frugally filling and very good.

zuppa di verdure

◯ SERVES 6   **🕐 PREP** 25 MINS, PLUS OVERNIGHT SOAKING   **❄ FREEZE** UP TO 3 MONTHS
COOK 2–3 HRS   BEFORE CAVOLO NERO IS ADDED

7oz (200g) dried cannellini beans, soaked
    overnight in water, or 1 x 14oz (400g) can
    cannellini beans, drained and rinsed
bouquet garni made from a sprig of rosemary,
    a sprig of thyme, and 2 bay leaves (see p24)
4 tbsp extra virgin olive oil, plus extra to serve
1 onion, chopped
3 carrots, diced
2 celery ribs, diced
2 leeks, very thinly sliced

3 garlic cloves, chopped
1 dried red chile pepper, finely chopped
3 tomatoes, peeled, seeded, and chopped
2 tbsp tomato purée
salt and freshly ground black pepper
4 cavolo nero or curly kale leaves, or the outer
    leaves of a Savoy cabbage, tough stalks
    removed and the leaves coarsely chopped
6 slices stale bread
1 garlic clove, cut in half

1 Drain the beans and place them in a large pan with the bouquet garni and twice their volume of cold water. Bring to a boil, then boil hard for 10 minutes. Lower the heat, and simmer gently for 1–2 hours or until tender, adding more water if needed. Remove the pan from the heat, discard the bouquet garni, and leave the beans to cool in their cooking water.

2 Heat the oil in a large heavy pot, then add the onion, carrots, celery, leeks, garlic, and chile. Cover with a lid and sweat over low heat for 10 minutes, stirring once or twice. Add the tomatoes and tomato purée and cook over a moderate heat for 3–4 minutes. Add the beans, their cooking water, and enough water to cover the vegetables generously. Season well with salt and pepper. Bring to a boil and simmer gently for 20 minutes or until the vegetables are tender. Purée half the soup in a blender, then return to the pan. Add the cavolo nero and simmer for 10 minutes or until tender. Adjust the seasonings.

3 Rub the bread with the garlic and arrange in a warm shallow casserole dish. Spoon in the soup and serve with a bottle of high-quality olive oil out on the table for people to help themselves.

Ribollita means "reboiled" in Italian, and that is more or less what this soup is—reboiled Zuppa di verdure (see left). It is wonderful, heart-warming comfort food.

ribollita

⊙ **SERVES** 4–6　　🕐 **PREP** 10 MINS **COOK** 40 MINS　　❄ **FREEZE** NOT SUITABLE

1 quantity day-old Zuppa di verdure, made up to the point just before the cavolo nero is added

6 cavolo nero or curly kale leaves, or the outer leaves of a Savoy cabbage, tough stalks removed and the leaves coarsely chopped

6 slices good-quality stale bread

1 garlic clove, halved

2–3 tbsp extra virgin olive oil, plus extra to serve

½–1 red onion, very finely sliced

4 tbsp freshly grated Parmesan (optional)

1 Preheat the oven to 375°F (190°C). Bring the soup to a boil in a large pan, stir in the cavolo nero, and simmer for 10 minutes or until tender. Meanwhile, rub the stale bread with garlic.

2 Oil a large gratin dish or similar ovenproof dish with olive oil, then spoon about a quarter of the soup into the dish, spreading it over the base. Now, lay half the slices of bread over the soup, then spoon over half the remaining soup. Repeat these two layers one more time. Lay the red onion over the top, then scatter with the Parmesan, if using. Drizzle over a little olive oil, then bake for 30 minutes. Serve sizzling hot, with extra olive oil out on the table for those that want it.

This one-pot meal of slowly cooked vegetables flavored with pork and confit of duck comes from southwest France. It is best made the day before and reheated.

garbure

⊘ **SERVES** 4–6   ◷ **PREP** 40 MINS **COOK** 1 HR   ✻ **FREEZE** UP TO 3 MONTHS

3½oz (100g) diced bacon or pancetta
1 Spanish onion, finely chopped
3 garlic cloves, crushed
1 leg confit of duck
1½ quarts (1½ liters) chicken stock
1 small Savoy cabbage, core removed and
  leaves cut into 1 x 3in (2.5 x 7.5cm) strips
1 large carrot, sliced
1 celery rib, diced
1 leek, cleaned and sliced
1 large floury potato, cubed

sea salt and freshly ground black pepper
1 tsp pimentón picante or hot
  smoked paprika
½ tsp ground cumin
2–3 sprigs of fresh thyme
2–3 sprigs of flat-leaf parsley, plus 1 tbsp
  finely chopped parsley to garnish
1 x 9oz (250g) can white beans, drained,
  rinsed, and drained again
8–12 croûtes (see p39), rubbed with garlic
  and brushed with olive oil, to serve

1 Put a large, deep, heavy-based soup pot over medium heat, add the bacon or pancetta, and cook, stirring frequently, for 2–3 minutes or until crisp and cooked through. Remove with a slotted spoon and drain on paper towels. Add the onion and garlic to the pot, reduce the heat a little, and cook, stirring frequently, for 5–8 minutes or until softened.

2 Pick the meat from the duck leg, discarding the skin and bones but reserving the fat, and cut into shreds. Stir the meat into the onion and garlic, then add the stock, cabbage, carrot, celery, leek, and potato. Season lightly with salt and more generously with freshly ground black pepper, then add the pimentón or paprika, cumin, thyme, and parsley. Bring to a simmer, cover, reduce the heat a little, and cook, stirring occasionally, for 30 minutes.

3 Lift out the thyme and parsley. Lightly mash the beans in a bowl, then stir them into the soup and continue cooking until the vegetables are tender. Taste and adjust the seasoning. To serve, stir in the reserved bacon or pancetta along with 1 tbsp of the duck fat, then sprinkle with the parsley. Place a croûte in each bowl and ladle the piping hot soup on top.

A mixed vegetable potage (soup) like this is traditional French family fare. It is ladled out of a tureen into wide shallow bowls as a starter all over the country.

french country soup

◎ SERVES 4   **◕ PREP** 15 MINS **COOK** 45 MINS   **✳ FREEZE** UP TO 3 MONTHS
AT THE END OF STEP 2

1 tbsp sunflower oil or peanut oil
2 tbsp butter
3 large leeks, cleaned and chopped
1 large floury potato, coarsely cubed
2 large carrots, chopped

3¼ cups vegetable stock or chicken stock
2 bay leaves
sea salt and freshly ground black pepper
½ cup hot water

1 Put the oil and half the butter in a large sauté pan over medium-low heat. Add the leeks, potato, and carrots and cook, stirring frequently, for 5 minutes. Reduce the heat a little, add the stock and bay leaves, then season lightly with salt and freshly ground black pepper. Cover and cook gently, stirring occasionally, for 30 minutes or until the vegetables are very soft.

2 Let cool for several minutes, then lift out the bay leaves. Transfer the soup to a blender and process until smooth. Strain back into the pan through a sieve, using the back of a wooden spoon to push through as much as possible. Pour the hot water through the sieve to extract as much as you can from the vegetables.

3 Reheat gently, stirring frequently. Taste and adjust the seasoning, then stir in the remaining butter and serve very hot.

POTATOES
Getting some of the less common varieties of potato is one of the great benefits of shopping at farmers' markets or belonging to a co-op or CSA. The same goes for many other kinds of vegetable, too.

Despite its French name, this silky-smooth, cold soup actually comes from the US. It is also delicious served hot—simply add the cream and chives at the end of cooking.

vichyssoise

SERVES 4   **PREP** 15 MINS, PLUS 3 HRS CHILLING   **FREEZE** UP TO 3 MONTHS
                 COOK 45 MINS   BEFORE THE CREAM IS ADDED

2 tbsp butter
3 large leeks (white parts only), finely sliced
2 potatoes, about 6oz (175g) in total, chopped
1 celery rib, coarsely chopped
4 cups hot vegetable stock

salt and freshly ground black pepper
5fl oz (150ml) heavy cream, plus extra
  to garnish
2 tbsp finely chopped chives

1 Melt the butter in a heavy pan over medium heat, add the leeks, and stir to coat well. Press a circle of damp wax paper on top of them, cover with a lid, and cook, shaking the pan gently from time to time, for 15 minutes or until they are soft and golden. Discard the wax paper.

2 Stir in the potatoes, celery, and stock, then season with salt and freshly ground black pepper. Bring to a boil, stirring all the time, then cover with a lid and simmer for 30 minutes or until the vegetables are tender.

3 Remove the pan from the heat and leave to cool slightly, then process the soup in a blender until very smooth. You may need to do this in batches. Season to taste with salt and freshly ground black pepper, then chill for at least 3 hours. To serve, pour into bowls, stir a little cream into each, then sprinkle with the chives and more freshly ground black pepper.

CHOOSING LEEKS
Although it means trimming and cleaning them, go for leeks with roots and plenty of green leaves rather than the neat cylinders you see in pre-prepared packs—it's hard to tell how fresh these are. For more information, see p23.

in praise of...
leeks

Leeks are regularly among the supporting cast in recipes, but on center stage, they are a revelation. Choose for tenderness and taste, then cook until they are soft; they are especially wonderful in soups.

This Parisian classic is given extra punch with a spoonful of brandy in every bowl. Serve it the moment you've made it—French onion soup is best piping hot.

french onion soup

SERVES 4   **PREP** 10 MINS **COOK** 1 HR 20 MINS   **FREEZE** UP TO 1 MONTH
WITHOUT THE CROÛTES AND CHEESE

2 tbsp butter
1 tbsp sunflower oil
1½lb (675g) onions, thinly sliced
1 tsp sugar
salt and freshly ground black pepper
½ cup red wine

2 tbsp plain flour
1½ quarts (1½ liters) hot beef stock
4 tbsp brandy
8 croûtes (see p39)
1 garlic clove, cut in half
4oz (115g) Gruyère or Emmental, grated

1 Melt the butter with the oil in a large, heavy pan over low heat. Add the onions and sugar and turn to coat well. Season with salt and freshly ground black pepper, then press a piece of damp wax paper on top of the onions. Cook, uncovered, stirring occasionally, for 40 minutes or until they are a rich dark brown color. Make sure that they do not stick and burn.

2 Remove the wax paper and stir in the wine. Increase the heat to medium and stir for 5 minutes while the onions glaze. Sprinkle in the flour and stir for 2 minutes, then pour in the stock and bring to a boil. Reduce the heat to low, cover with a lid, and let simmer for 30 minutes. Taste and season with salt and freshly ground black pepper, if necessary.

3 Preheat the grill to its highest setting. Divide the soup among flameproof bowls and stir 1 tbsp of the brandy into each. Rub the croûtes with the cut garlic and place one in each bowl. Sprinkle with the cheese and grill for 2–3 minutes or until the cheese is bubbling and golden. Serve at once.

Meltingly soft onions make a flavorful base for this lightly spiced soup enriched with almonds and sweetened with a hint of caramel.

onion and almond soup

⊘ SERVES 4   **⏱ PREP** 20 MINS, PLUS 2 HOURS SALTING   **❄ FREEZE** UP TO 2 MONTHS
                     COOK 1 HR   BEFORE HALF-AND-HALF IS ADDED

1 onion, very finely sliced
½ tsp sea salt
vegetable oil, to deep-fry
3½oz (100g) almonds (with skins on)
3¼ cups hot chicken stock
4 tbsp butter
¼ tsp nigella seeds

4 large onions, diced
1 red chile, chopped
1 tsp dark brown (muscovado) sugar
2 tbsp balsamic vinegar
½ cup half-and-half
salt and freshly ground black pepper

1 For a fried onion garnish, put the onion slices in a shallow dish, sprinkle with the sea salt, then set to one side for at least 2 hours. Using your hands, squeeze out the liquid, then pat dry with paper towels. Deep-fry in hot oil for 1–2 minutes or until golden, then drain on paper towels.

2 Bring a small pan of water to a boil, add the almonds, turn off the heat, and cover with a lid. Let soak for 15 minutes, then drain and slip off the skins once the nuts are cool enough to handle. Transfer to a food processor with ½ cup of the stock, then process to a paste and set aside.

3 Meanwhile, melt the butter in a large pan, add the nigella seeds, and cook over low heat for 1 minute. Stir in the diced onions and chile, cover, and cook over very low heat for 20–30 minutes or until soft but not brown, then turn up the heat and remove the lid. When the onions begin to turn golden in color, stir in the sugar and cook until it starts sticking to the bottom of the pan. Add the vinegar and continue cooking until sticky.

4 Add the rest of the stock and the almond paste and simmer for 20 minutes. Process the soup until smooth in a blender, then return to the pan, stir in the cream, and season with salt and freshly ground black pepper. Reheat gently and serve garnished with the fried onions.

If you can't find fresh chanterelle mushrooms for this, you can use jarred or canned. Drain, rinse, and then drain them again before you cook them.

german potato soup

SERVES 6   **PREP** 25 MINS **COOK** 45 MINS   **FREEZE** UP TO 3 MONTHS
WITHOUT ONIONS AND MUSHROOMS

5 tbsp butter
¼ celeriac, diced
9oz (250g) carrots, diced
1½lb (675g) floury potatoes, diced
1 onion, studded with a bay leaf and a clove
1½ quarts (1½ liters) hot vegetable stock
7oz (200g) leeks, sliced
1 onion, diced

7oz (200g) chanterelles, large ones halved
½ cup heavy whipping cream or
 ⅔ cup crème fraîche
salt and freshly ground black pepper
pinch of dried marjoram
pinch of freshly grated nutmeg
2 tbsp chopped flat-leaf parsley, chervil,
 or chives

1 Melt 3 tbsp of the butter in a large pan, add the celeriac and carrots, and cook, stirring frequently, for 6–8 minutes or until light brown. Add the potatoes, onion, and stock and bring to a boil. Lower the heat, cover with a lid, and simmer for 20 minutes or until tender. Add the leeks, cover again, and cook for 10 minutes more.

2 Meanwhile, melt the rest of the butter in a frying pan, add the diced onion, and cook, stirring continuously, for 4–5 minutes or until soft but not brown. Add the chanterelles and cook, stirring frequently, for 5 minutes.

3 Remove the whole onion from the soup and discard. Transfer about one-third of the contents of the pan to a blender and process until smooth. Stir in the cream and return to the pan. Season with salt and freshly ground black pepper, then add the marjoram, nutmeg, and the cooked onion and chanterelles, and reheat gently. Serve sprinkled with the herbs over the top.

The scallops are a counterpoint to the distinctive taste of the Jerusalem artichoke purée in this traditional soup menu pairing.

scallop and artichoke soup

◉ SERVES 4   **🕐 PREP** 20 MINS **COOK** 25 MINS   **❄ FREEZE** UP TO 3 MONTHS
AT THE END OF STEP 1

7 tbsp unsalted butter
1 onion, chopped
1 garlic clove, chopped
2¼lb (1kg) Jerusalem artichokes, peeled or scrubbed and cut into small dice
1½ quarts (1½ liters) hot chicken stock or water
½ cup heavy cream

salt and freshly ground black pepper
a pinch of freshly grated nutmeg
4 thick slices bacon, cut into small dice
4 scallops
2 tbsp sunflower oil
few drops of lemon juice
snipped chives, to garnish

1 Melt 3½ tbsp butter in a large pan and cook the onion gently. Add the garlic and artichokes and sweat over low heat for 3 minutes. Add the stock or water, cover with a lid, and simmer until the artichokes are completely cooked and soft. Purée in a blender with the cream and the remaining butter. You may need to do this in batches. Return to the pan and season with salt and freshly ground black pepper, then sprinkle in the nutmeg and keep warm.

2 Cook the bacon in a frying pan until crisp, then spoon on to paper towels to drain. Season the scallops with salt and freshly ground black pepper, then cook quickly in the sunflower oil—they will be ready almost as soon as they are sealed by the heat. Squeeze a few drops of lemon juice over the top.

3 Divide the artichoke purée among four bowls, spoon the bacon and scallops on top, then garnish with the chives and serve.

Use whatever proportion of carrots and Jerusalem artichokes you have, adding up to 1lb 9oz (700g) in total. The carrots enhance the color and sweetness of the soup.

jerusalem artichoke soup with saffron and thyme

◉ SERVES 4–6   **◐ PREP** 15 MINS **COOK** 35–45 MINS   **✳ FREEZE** UP TO 3 MONTHS

2 tbsp extra-virgin olive oil, plus extra
   to garnish
2 medium onions, chopped
3 garlic cloves, chopped
12oz (350g) Jerusalem artichokes, scrubbed
   and coarsely chopped
12oz (350g) carrots, scrubbed and
   coarsely chopped

sea salt and freshly ground black pepper
1.2 quarts (1.2 liters) hot vegetable stock
1 tbsp fresh thyme leaves or
   1½ tsp dried thyme
large pinch (about 30 strands) of saffron
juice of ½ lemon

1 Heat the oil in a large pan over medium heat, add the onions, and cook for 5–10 minutes or until soft and translucent. Add the garlic and cook for another 30 seconds or until fragrant. Stir in the artichokes, carrots, and a little salt, then cover with a lid and sweat, stirring frequently, for 10–15 minutes or until the vegetables are softened.

2 Add the stock, thyme, and saffron, bring to a boil, then lower the heat to a simmer and cook for 20 minutes or until the vegetables are thoroughly soft. Cool briefly, then process until smooth in a blender. Stir in the lemon juice and season to taste with salt and freshly ground black pepper. Serve in warm bowls, with a drizzle of olive oil on top.

Make the effort to cook up your own stock, as the flavor of the celeriac and hazelnuts in this pale, creamy soup is not strong enough to disguise any shortcomings.

celeriac and hazelnut soup

SERVES 6   **PREP** 15 MINS **COOK** 40 MINS   ✱ **FREEZE** UP TO 3 MONTHS
WITHOUT LEMON JUICE AND CREAM

3½oz (100g) shelled hazelnuts
3 tbsp butter
1 medium–large celeriac, coarsely diced
1 onion, chopped
2 tbsp long- or short-grain rice

1 quart (1 liter) hot chicken stock
salt and freshly ground black pepper
juice of ½ lemon
½ cup heavy cream

1 Preheat the oven to 375°F (190°C). Spread the hazelnuts out on a baking sheet and roast for 5–10 minutes or until they turn a shade darker and the skins flake off easily. Check regularly to prevent burning. Let them cool slightly, then rub off the skins.

2 Melt the butter in a large pan over low heat. Add the celeriac, onion, rice, and hazelnuts, turn to coat well, then cover and let sweat gently for 10–15 minutes, stirring once or twice. Pour in half the stock, season well with salt and freshly ground black pepper, and bring to a boil. Simmer gently for 15 minutes or until the celeriac and rice are tender.

3 Let the soup cool for a few minutes, then process until completely smooth in a blender, adding the remaining stock to thin the soup down. Return to the pan, stir in the lemon juice and then the cream, and reheat, being sure to taste and balance the seasoning. Serve hot and steaming.

A light, colorful soup with quite a kick from the jalapeño. Large turnips have a stronger flavor, which is perfect for this dish. Don't use delicate baby ones.

spicy turnip soup with pimento and noodles

🍲 **SERVES** 4–6   🕐 **PREP** 10 MINS **COOK** 30 MINS   ❄ **FREEZE** UP TO 3 MONTHS
AT THE END OF STEP 1

4 scallions, chopped
2 good-sized turnips, diced
½ tsp crushed hot red pepper flakes
1 green jalapeño pepper, seeded
  and cut into thin rings
2 star anise
2 tsp tomato purée

1 quart (1 liter) hot vegetable stock or
  light chicken stock
1 package dried thin Chinese egg noodles
1 preserved pimento, drained and diced
1–2 tsp soy sauce, to taste
freshly ground black pepper
small handful of cilantro, torn

1 Put the scallions, turnips, pepper flakes, jalapeño, star anise, tomato purée, and stock in a saucepan and bring to a boil. Lower the heat, partially cover with a lid, and simmer gently for 30 minutes or until the turnips are very tender. Discard the star anise.

2 Meanwhile, put the noodles in a bowl, cover with boiling water, and let stand for 5 minutes, stirring to loosen, then drain. Stir the noodles into the soup, along with the pimento. Season to taste with soy sauce and freshly ground black pepper, then stir in half the cilantro. Ladle into warm soup bowls, top with the remaining cilantro, and serve.

TURNIPS
Choose organic turnips for the sweetest, most mustardy flavor. To prepare, trim. Small turnips then need only the thinnest layer of skin peeled off. Larger turnips, however, usually have a thicker layer of hard woody skin to peel.

Alice Waters of Chez Panisse restaurant in California writes, "young turnips with their greens are in the markets in spring and fall. Together they make a delicious soup."

turnip soup

⊘ **SERVES** 4–6   🕐 **PREP** 20 MINS **COOK** 40 MINS   ❄ **FREEZE** UP TO 3 MONTHS

2 bunches of young turnips with greens,
   about 1½lb (675g) total in weight
3 tbsp butter or olive oil
1 onion, thinly sliced
1 bay leaf

2 sprigs of thyme
sea salt
1¼ quarts (1¼ liters) well-flavored
   chicken stock

1 Remove the greens from the turnips, then trim and discard the stems. Rinse and drain the leaves and cut into ½in (1cm) strips. Trim the roots from the bases and, if the skins are tough (taste one to see), peel before slicing thinly. Heat the butter or oil in a heavy pot over low heat, add the onion, and cook very gently for 12 minutes or until soft.

2 Stir in the turnip bases, along with the bay leaf and thyme, and season with salt. Cook for 5 minutes, stirring occasionally, then pour in the stock and bring to a boil. Lower the heat to a simmer, cover, and cook for 10 minutes. Add the turnip greens and cook for another 5–10 minutes or until tender. Remove the bay leaf, check the seasoning, and serve. This is excellent with a little grated Parmesan on top.

Aromatic spicing balances the natural sweetness of the parsnips in this warming soup. Beef stock will give the best flavor, but chicken or vegetable stock can also be used.

curried parsnip soup

⊘ **SERVES** 4　　🕐 **PREP** 25 MINS **COOK** 30 MINS　　❄ **FREEZE** UP TO 3 MONTHS
BEFORE CREAM IS ADDED

1 heaped tbsp coriander seeds
1 tsp cumin seeds
1 dried red chile or ½ tsp crushed
　hot red pepper flakes
1 rounded tsp ground turmeric
¼ tsp ground fenugreek
1 medium onion, chopped
1 large garlic clove, split in half

1½lb (675g) parsnips, cored and diced
2 tbsp butter
1 tbsp flour
1 quart (1 liter) vegetable stock, beef stock,
　or chicken stock
salt and freshly ground black pepper
⅔ cup heavy cream
chopped chives or parsley, to garnish

1 Process the first five ingredients in a coffee grinder, or pound the whole spices in a mortar, then mix with the ground. Transfer the mixture to a small jar—you will not need all of it for this recipe.

2 Cook the onion, garlic, and parsnips gently in the butter, lid on the pan, for 10 minutes. Stir in the flour and 1–2 tbsp of the spice mixture. Cook for 2 minutes, stirring from time to time. Pour in the stock gradually, stirring constantly. Bring to a boil and let simmer gently for 10–15 minutes or until the parsnips are really tender.

3 Purée until smooth in a blender, then dilute to taste with water. Season to taste with salt and freshly ground black pepper, then reheat. Add the cream and serve with the chives or parsley scattered over the top.

PARSNIPS
Widely produced organically, parsnips should be heavy for their size, with firm, unblemished skin. To prepare, trim the ends, then peel thinly. Baby parsnips can be cooked whole, while larger ones should be sliced and diced.

The sweetness of the parsnip is balanced by mild curry powder and sharp green apple in this easy-to-prepare and warming, smooth winter soup.

parsnip and apple soup

SERVES 4   **PREP** 20 MINS **COOK** 30 MINS   **FREEZE** UP TO 3 MONTHS
WITHOUT CREAM AND LEMON JUICE

1 tbsp olive oil
½ tbsp butter
½ Spanish onion, finely chopped
1 garlic clove, crushed
2 tsp mild curry powder
2¼lb (1kg) parsnips, chopped
sea salt and freshly ground black pepper

1 large Granny Smith apple, peeled, cored, and chopped
1 quart (1 liter) hot vegetable stock or light chicken stock
6 tbsp half-and-half
2 tbsp lemon juice

1 Heat the oil and butter in a large sauté pan over low heat. Add the onion, garlic, and curry powder and cook gently, stirring frequently, for 2–3 minutes or until the onion has softened. Add the parsnips and season lightly with salt and freshly ground black pepper. Turn the heat up a little and cook, stirring frequently, for 5 minutes or until the parsnips are golden.

2 Add the apple, stir for 1 minute, then pour in the stock and bring to a boil. Lower the heat and simmer for 10–12 minutes or until the parsnips are tender. Take off the heat and let cool for several minutes, then transfer to a blender or food processor and process until smooth and creamy.

3 Pass the soup through a sieve placed over the pan, then rinse out the blender or food processor with ½ cup hot water and stir this into the soup. Reheat gently, then stir in the half-and half and lemon juice. Adjust the seasoning and serve piping hot.

The vegetables for this soup are cooked in the oven, which brings out their naturally sweet flavor. This is delicious served with warm pita bread.

moroccan roasted sweet potato soup

SERVES 4   **PREP** 20 MINS **COOK** 50 MINS   **FREEZE** UP TO 3 MONTHS
BEFORE THE YOGURT IS ADDED

1½lb (675g) sweet potatoes, cut into big chunks
6 large shallots, quartered
3 plump garlic cloves, unpeeled
1 carrot, cut into large chunks
1 tbsp harissa, plus extra to serve
2 tbsp olive oil

salt and freshly ground black pepper
1 quart (1 liter) hot vegetable stock
1 tsp honey
generous squeeze of lemon juice
natural yogurt, to serve
warm pita bread, to serve

1 Preheat the oven to 400°F (200°C). Place the sweet potatoes, shallots, garlic, and carrot in a roasting pan. Mix the harissa with the oil, then pour over the vegetables and toss together so they are all well coated. Season with freshly ground black pepper, then roast, turning occasionally, for 40 minutes or until tender and turning golden. Remove from the oven.

2 Squeeze the garlic out of their skins into the roasting pan. Stir in the stock and honey, then scrape up all the bits from the bottom of the pan. Carefully transfer to a blender and process until smooth. You may need to do this in batches. Pour into a saucepan and reheat gently.

3 Add a good squeeze of lemon juice and season to taste with salt and freshly ground black pepper. Swirl the yogurt with a little harissa and top each bowl with a spoonful. Serve with warm pita bread.

A thick, creamy soup with an amazing vivid orange color. If you are using a stock cube, be sure to taste the soup before adding any extra salt.

pumpkin soup

SERVES 6   **PREP** 10 MINS **COOK** 20 MINS   **FREEZE** UP TO 3 MONTHS
WITHOUT THE SAGE GARNISH

1 small pumpkin (or part of a large one), about 1lb 10oz (750g) in total, peeled and cubed
2 medium potatoes, peeled and cubed
1 tbsp olive oil
2½ cups vegetable stock
2 tomatoes, chopped

4 fresh sage leaves
sea salt and freshly ground black pepper

for the garnish
olive oil, for frying
18 large fresh sage leaves

1 Heat the oil in a saucepan and cook the pumpkin and potatoes for 5 minutes. Add the stock, chopped tomatoes, and the 4 sage leaves. Cover and simmer for about 10 minutes, until the vegetables are soft.

2 Using a blender, process the soup until smooth, then gently reheat. Season with salt and pepper, to taste.

3 For the garnish, heat a little oil in a frying pan and, once hot, fry the large sage leaves until crisp. Scatter the crispy leaves over the soup and serve immediately.

This recipe first appeared in *Fork to Fork* by Monty and Sarah Don, published by Conran Octopus and reproduced by kind permission

You can cook the apples—skin, core, and all—as you will be sieving the end result. For special occasions, use dry sherry or white wine instead of water.

pumpkin and apple soup

SERVES 6   **PREP** 20 MINS **COOK** 40 MINS   ❄ **FREEZE** UP TO 3 MONTHS

4 tbsp unsalted butter
1 medium onion, finely chopped
7oz (200g) pumpkin flesh, diced
2 sharp-tasting apples such as
   Granny Smith, diced

½ cup hot water
4 cups cold vegetable stock or
   chicken stock
salt and freshly ground black pepper
2 tsp toasted pumpkin seeds, to garnish

1 Melt the butter in a large saucepan, add the onion, and cook very gently, stirring often, for 10 minutes or until soft. Do not let it brown. Add the pumpkin and apples and stir to coat well. Pour in the hot water, cover with a lid, and leave on a very, very low heat for 30 minutes, stirring from time to time. If the liquid evaporates, pour in a little more hot water. The vegetables and fruit should be very soft at the end of cooking.

2 Stir in the stock, then blend the soup in batches. As each batch is done, pour it into a sieve set over a clean saucepan. Press the contents through with the back of a ladle, a wooden spoon, or a pestle.

3 When all the soup has been sieved, reheat it very gently, then season to taste with salt and freshly ground black pepper. Serve garnished with the toasted pumpkin seeds.

This is an unexpectedly good soup, with all the fresh, nutty flavor of Brussels sprouts tempered by the natural sweetness of the onion.

brussels sprout soup

⬤ **SERVES** 4–6   🕐 **PREP** 20 MINS **COOK** 1 HR 10 MINS   ❄ **FREEZE** UP TO 3 MONTHS
WITHOUT THE SOUR CREAM

1lb (450g) onions, sliced
2 tbsp butter
1 tbsp sugar
1lb (450g) Brussels sprouts, trimmed
  and halved
1 generous sprig thyme

1¼ quarts (1¼ liters) chicken or
  vegetable stock
salt and freshly ground black pepper
sour cream, crème fraîche, or
  Greek-style yogurt, to serve
paprika or cayenne pepper, to serve

1 Place the onions in a pan with the butter. Cover and cook over low heat for about 30–40 minutes until the onions are incredibly tender and soft. Sprinkle in the sugar and cook, uncovered, for another 10–15 minutes or so until the onions are lightly colored and concentrated, stirring occasionally.

2 Add the sprouts and the thyme and stir. Pour in the stock and season with salt and pepper. Bring to a boil and simmer for 10–15 minutes until the sprouts are just tender. Cool slightly, remove the thyme, and process in two batches. Reheat gently if needed, then taste and adjust the seasoning. Serve piping hot, with a spoonful of sour cream, crème fraîche, or yogurt in each bowlful, and a light dusting of paprika or cayenne.

BRUSSELS SPROUTS
Look for locally grown sprouts. They can range from the size of a thumbnail to a golf ball, but smaller equals sweeter. Before using home-grown sprouts, soak them in cold water, as they may contain a few worms.

This earthy soup combines mildly nutty celeriac and more assertive celery to create a fragrant, satisfying winter warmer.

n celery and celeriac soup

⊘ **SERVES** 4   🕐 **PREP** 15 MINS **COOK** 20 MINS   ❄ **FREEZE** UP TO 3 MONTHS
                                                                    WITHOUT THE CHILLED BUTTER

1 tbsp sunflower, peanut, or mild-flavored
  olive oil
2 tbsp butter
1lb 2oz (500g) celeriac, peeled and chopped
1 large head celery, cored and chopped
1 medium floury potato, peeled and chopped

sea salt and freshly ground black pepper
1 quart (1 liter) vegetable stock or
  chicken stock
2 tbsp chilled butter, diced
4 slices walnut bread, lightly toasted,
  to serve

1 Put the oil and 2 tbsp butter in a large sauté pan over medium heat. Add the celeriac, celery, and potato. Stir well for 2–3 minutes then reduce the heat a little. Add 3–4 tbsp water, and season lightly. Partially cover and let stew gently until very soft. Stir the vegetables from time to time and keep the heat low.

2 Transfer the cooked vegetables to a food processor and purée. Return to the pan and add the stock. Season, stir briskly to blend, and bring to a simmer over medium heat, stirring frequently. Reduce the heat a little and let simmer gently for 10–15 minutes, still stirring occasionally. Taste and adjust the seasoning.

3 Just before serving, whisk in the chilled diced butter. Serve hot with toasted walnut bread.

CELERY
Most celery found in markets is naturally vibrantly green, but look out for the less bitter blanched white variety, too. Celery's thick outer stalks are best in soups, stews, and casseroles, rather than eaten raw.

This hearty Italian country soup has deep, earthy flavors. Check the mushrooms after soaking, because there may be bits of dirt or straw that need to be removed.

porcini mushroom soup

SERVES 4   **PREP** 20 MINS, PLUS 30 MINS STANDING **COOK** 1 HR   **FREEZE** UP TO 3 MONTHS WITHOUT THE BREAD

1oz (30g) dried porcini mushrooms
3 tbsp extra virgin olive oil, plus extra
  to serve
2 onions, finely chopped
2 tsp chopped fresh rosemary leaves
1 tsp fresh thyme leaves
2 garlic cloves, finely sliced

4oz (115g) chestnut mushrooms, sliced
2 celery ribs with leaves, finely chopped
1 x 14oz (400g) can chopped tomatoes
3¼ cups vegetable stock
salt and freshly ground black pepper
½ stale ciabatta or small crusty white loaf,
  torn into chunks

1 Put the dried porcini in a heatproof bowl, pour over 1¼ cups boiling water, and let stand for 30 minutes. Drain, reserving the soaking liquid, then chop any large pieces of porcini.

2 Heat the oil in a saucepan, add the onions, cover, and let cook for 10 minutes, or until soft. Add the rosemary, thyme, garlic, chestnut mushrooms, and celery, and continue cooking, uncovered, until the celery has softened.

3 Add the tomatoes, porcini, and the stock. Strain the soaking liquid through a piece of muslin or a fine sieve into the pan. Bring the soup to a boil, then lower the heat and simmer gently for 45 minutes.

4 Season to taste with salt and pepper, and add the chunks of bread. Remove the pan from the heat. Cover and let stand for 10 minutes before serving. Spoon into deep bowls and drizzle each serving with a little olive oil.

in praise of...

mushrooms

Nothing is more satisfying to a cook than a mushroom soup: first the foraging in the woods or choosing the best specimens from the market; then the making of the dish, and finally the eating.

Using a selection of both wild and cultivated mushrooms produces a soup bursting with flavor. The horseradish cream provides a welcome kick.

mushroom soup

SERVES 4   **PREP** 10 MINS **COOK** 45 MINS   ❄ **FREEZE** UP TO 3 MONTHS

2 tbsp butter
1 onion, finely chopped
2 celery ribs, finely chopped
1 garlic clove, crushed
1lb (450g) mixed mushrooms,
  coarsely chopped

7oz (200g) potatoes, peeled and cubed
1 quart (1 liter) vegetable stock
2 tbsp finely chopped fresh parsley
salt and freshly ground black pepper
horseradish cream, to serve (optional)

1 Melt the butter in a large saucepan, add the onion, celery, and garlic, and cook for 3–4 minutes, or until softened.

2 Stir in the mushrooms and continue to cook for another 5–6 minutes. Add the potatoes and the stock, and bring to a boil. Reduce the heat and let simmer gently for 30 minutes.

3 Using a blender, process the soup until smooth, working in batches if necessary. Sprinkle the parsley over the top and season to taste with salt and pepper. Serve immediately, stirring a little horseradish cream into each soup bowl, if desired, for an extra kick.

legumes and nuts

This hearty, substantial soup improves with reheating, so it benefits from being made a day in advance. Reheat gently over low heat.

tuscan bean soup

SERVES 4   **PREP** 15 MINS **COOK** 1 HR 20 MINS   **FREEZE** UP TO 3 MONTHS

4 tbsp extra virgin olive oil, plus extra for drizzling
1 onion, chopped
2 carrots, sliced
1 leek, sliced
2 garlic cloves, chopped
1 x 14oz (400g) can chopped tomatoes
1 tbsp tomato purée
1 quart (1 liter) chicken stock

salt and freshly ground black pepper
1 x 14oz (400g) can borlotti beans, navy beans, or cannellini beans, drained and rinsed
9oz (250g) baby spinach leaves or spring greens, shredded
8 slices ciabatta bread
grated Parmesan cheese, for sprinkling

1 Heat the oil in a large saucepan and cook the onion, carrot, and leek over low heat for 10 minutes, or until softened but not colored. Add the garlic and cook for 1 minute. Add the tomatoes, tomato purée, and stock. Season to taste with salt and pepper.

2 Mash half the beans with a fork and add to the pan. Bring to a boil, then lower the heat and simmer for 30 minutes. Add the remaining beans and spinach to the pan. Simmer for another 30 minutes.

3 Toast the bread until golden, place 2 pieces in each soup bowl, and drizzle with olive oil. To serve, spoon the soup into the bowls, top with a sprinkling of Parmesan, and drizzle with a little more olive oil.

Robust, garlicky, and fragrant with rosemary and sage, this is a hearty, satisfying soup. Serve it with some fresh crusty bread and a drizzle of good-quality olive oil.

bean and rosemary soup

SERVES 8   **PREP** 15 MINS **COOK** 40 MINS   ✻ **FREEZE** UP TO 3 MONTHS

2 tbsp olive oil
2 onions, finely chopped
salt and freshly ground black pepper
1 tbsp finely chopped fresh rosemary leaves
a few fresh sage leaves, finely chopped
4 celery ribs, finely chopped

3 garlic cloves, grated or finely chopped
2 tbsp tomato purée
2 x 14oz (400g) cans borlotti beans, drained,
   rinsed, and drained again
1¼ quarts (1¼ liters) hot chicken stock
5½lb (2.5kg) potatoes, cut into chunky pieces

1 Heat the oil in a large pan, add the onions, and cook over low heat for 6–8 minutes or until soft and translucent. Season well with salt and freshly ground black pepper, then stir in the rosemary, sage, celery, and garlic and cook over very low heat, stirring occasionally, for 10 minutes.

2 Stir in the tomato purée and beans and cook gently for 5 minutes. Pour in the stock, bring to a boil, then add the potatoes and simmer gently for 15 minutes or until cooked. Taste, season with salt and freshly ground black pepper, if needed, and serve.

This is so thick and hearty it is a meal in itself—a real family soup. For children, try topping it with some broken-up tortilla chips.

mexican chili bean soup

🔘 **SERVES** 4   🕐 **PREP** 10 MINS **COOK** 40 MINS   ❄️ **FREEZE** UP TO 3 MONTHS
AT THE END OF STEP 2

2 tbsp sunflower oil
1 onion, chopped
1 small red bell pepper, seeded and
    finely chopped
2 garlic cloves, finely chopped
14oz (400g) lean ground beef
1 tsp ground cumin
2 tsp medium or hot chili powder
½ tsp dried oregano
1 x 14oz (400g) can chopped plum tomatoes

2 tbsp tomato purée
3¼ cups hot vegetable stock
    or chicken stock
1 x 14oz (400g) can red kidney beans,
    drained, rinsed, and drained again
handful of chopped flat-leaf parsley
salt and freshly ground black pepper
sour cream or natural yogurt, to serve
grated Cheddar, to serve
4 warm tortillas (optional), to serve

1 Heat the oil in a large saucepan, add the onion, and cook for 5 minutes. Add the pepper and garlic and stir-fry for 2 minutes. Add the beef and stir-fry for 5 minutes or until it has broken up and browned. Stir in the cumin, chili powder, and oregano and cook for another minute or so.

2 Stir in the tomatoes, tomato purée, and stock, then simmer for about 20–25 minutes or until reduced slightly and a good soupy consistency. Add the beans and simmer for another 5 minutes. Stir in half the parsley and season with salt and freshly ground black pepper.

3 Ladle into bowls and serve topped with a spoonful of sour cream or yogurt, a scattering of Cheddar, and the rest of the parsley.

RED KIDNEY BEANS
Valued for their color and the robust, sweet flavor they acquire during cooking, red kidney beans are sometimes known as chili beans. When buying them canned, go for organic beans preserved without salt or sugar.

This hearty, wholesome soup takes the edge off chilly winter weather. It's worth using dried beans, which have a much fuller flavor than the canned variety.

creamy kidney bean soup

⊘ SERVES 6   **🕐 PREP** 20 MINS **COOK** 3¼ HRS   **❄ FREEZE** UP TO 3 MONTHS
                    OR 30 MINS IN A PRESSURE COOKER   AT THE END OF STEP 3

8oz (225g) dried kidney beans, soaked
   overnight in cold water
2 red onions, diced
1 x 14oz (400g) can chopped tomatoes
1 tbsp tomato purée
5 garlic cloves, halved
2in (5cm) fresh ginger, coarsely chopped
3 large green chiles, left whole
salt and freshly ground black pepper

⅔ cup half-and-half
squeeze of fresh lime juice, to taste

for the garnish
4–6 red radishes, sliced
1 large green chile, finely chopped
2 tbsp chopped fresh cilantro leaves
squeeze of fresh lime juice, to taste

1 Drain the kidney beans, discarding the soaking liquid. Put the beans in a very large heavy-bottomed pan and cover with 1¾ quarts (1¾ liters) of water. Add the onions, tomatoes, tomato purée, garlic, ginger, and chiles and bring to a boil.

2 Cover the pan, lower the heat, and simmer for about 3 hours, until the beans are just breaking up. Add more liquid if needed during cooking. You could also use a pressure cooker—the beans will be tender in about 30 minutes.

3 Once the beans have cooled slightly, scoop out the chiles. Using a blender, process the soup in batches until smooth, then sieve to remove the skins. Season well with salt and pepper.

4 Stir in the half-and-half, and reheat. Add lime juice to taste. For the garnish, combine the sliced radish with the green chile and cilantro. Sharpen with a squeeze of lime, then top each bowl of soup with a small heap of the thin radishes.

This thick soup from northern Italy is guaranteed to keep out the winter chills. Soak the beans overnight to rehydrate them and cut down on the cooking time.

white bean soup

SERVES 4   **PREP** 30 MINS **COOK** 2 HRS   ✳ **FREEZE** UP TO 3 MONTHS
AT THE END OF STEP 3

3 tbsp olive oil
2 onions, finely chopped
2 garlic cloves, crushed
8oz (225g) dried cannellini beans,
 soaked overnight
1 celery rib, chopped
1 bay leaf
3–4 parsley stems, without leaves

1 tbsp lemon juice
1¼ quarts (1¼ liters) vegetable stock
salt and freshly ground black pepper
3 shallots, thinly sliced
2oz (60g) pancetta, chopped (optional)
3oz (85g) Fontina or Taleggio cheese,
 chopped into small pieces

1 Heat 2 tbsp olive oil in a saucepan, add the onions, and cook over low heat for 10 minutes, or until softened, stirring occasionally. Add the garlic and cook, stirring, for 1 minute.

2 Drain the soaked beans and add to the pan with the celery, bay leaf, parsley stems, lemon juice, and stock. Bring to a boil, cover, and simmer for 1½ hours, or until the beans are soft, stirring occasionally.

3 Remove the bay leaf and process the soup in batches in a blender, or through a hand mill. Rinse out the pan. Return the soup to the pan and season to taste with salt and pepper.

4 Heat the remaining olive oil in a small frying pan, and cook the shallots and pancetta (if using) until golden and crisp, stirring frequently to keep them from sticking to the pan. Reheat the soup, adding a little stock or water if it is too thick. Stir the Fontina into the soup. Ladle into individual bowls, and sprinkle each serving with the shallots and pancetta.

Navy beans give texture while rosemary and dried mushrooms provide loads of flavor for this rustic Italian-style soup.

rosemary's bean soup with italian cheese crisps

SERVES 4   **PREP** 10 MINS PLUS 20 MINS SOAKING **COOK** 15–20 MINS   **FREEZE** UP TO 3 MONTHS WITHOUT CHEESE CRISPS

½oz (12g) dried porcini mushrooms, covered in water to soak
1¾oz (50g) pecorino or Parmesan cheese, coarsely grated
1½ tsp very finely chopped rosemary
2 tbsp olive oil
1 onion, chopped

2 garlic cloves, chopped
3 rosemary sprigs
2 x 14oz (400g) cans navy (or flageolet) beans, drained and rinsed
2½ cups vegetable stock
extra virgin olive oil, for drizzling
ciabatta loaf cut into chunks, to serve

1 Preheat the oven to 400°F (200°C). Let the mushrooms soak for 20 minutes. Meanwhile, make the cheese crisps. Line a baking sheet with parchment paper. Scatter the cheese and half the rosemary in a thin, even layer on the sheet in an 7in (18cm) circle. Bake for 8 minutes or until it starts to turn golden around the edges. Remove and let cool and firm on the sheet. Strain the mushrooms (reserving the liquid) and coarsely chop.

2 Heat the oil in a large saucepan, add the onion, and soften for 4–5 minutes. Stir in the garlic, chopped mushrooms, and rosemary. Cook for 2–3 minutes. Add the beans, stock, and 6 tbsp of the reserved mushroom liquid. Simmer for 10 minutes. Remove the rosemary. Coarsely purée about three-quarters of the soup. Pour this back into the pan with the rest of the soup. Season to taste with salt and pepper, then warm through.

3 Break the cheese crisps into large pieces. For each serving, sprinkle with the rest of the chopped rosemary, drizzle with the oil, and accompany with the cheese crisps and ciabatta.

Lime gives a distinctive, vibrant twist to this clean-tasting, healthy soup from New Mexico. It has the added advantage of being very quick and easy to prepare.

green lentil soup with lime

 SERVES 4   **PREP** 5 MINS **COOKING** 30 MINS   **FREEZE** UP TO 3 MONTHS
                                                                         AT THE END OF STEP 3

1 quart (1 liter) chicken stock
2–3 sprigs fresh thyme
10oz (300g) green lentils

sea salt and freshly ground black pepper
grated zest and juice of 1 organic lime

1 Pour the stock into a saucepan over medium heat. Add the thyme and bring to a simmer.

2 Add the lentils, and season lightly with salt and pepper. Return to a simmer, cover, reduce the heat a little. Cook for 20–25 minutes until the lentils are very soft.

3 Turn off the heat and let cool for several minutes. Transfer to a blender or food processor, and process until just smooth.

4 Pour the soup back into the saucepan and stir in the lime zest and juice. Reheat gently, taste, and adjust the seasoning. Serve very hot.

This hearty vegetarian soup has just a touch of spice and is quick and easy to prepare. Serve with plain, low-fat yogurt and good crusty bread.

lentil soup

SERVES 4   **PREP** 20 MINS **COOK** 35 MINS   **FREEZE** UP TO 3 MONTHS

1 tbsp olive oil
2 onions, finely chopped
2 celery ribs, finely chopped
2 carrots, finely chopped
2 garlic cloves, crushed

1–2 tsp curry powder
5½oz (150g) red lentils
1½ quarts (1½ liters) vegetable stock
½ cup tomato or vegetable juice
salt and freshly ground black pepper

1 Heat the oil in a large pan over medium heat, then add the onions, celery, and carrots. Cook, stirring, for 5 minutes, or until the onions are soft and translucent.

2 Add the garlic and curry powder and cook, stirring, for another minute, then add the lentils, stock, and tomato juice.

3 Bring to a boil, then lower the heat, cover, and simmer for 25 minutes, or until the vegetables are tender. Season to taste with salt and pepper, and serve hot.

This Moroccan bean and lentil soup is a meal in a bowl often eaten for breakfast during Ramadan, to keep people going right through a day of fasting.

harira

⊘ **SERVES** 6–8   🕐 **PREP** 15 MINS **COOK** 1 HR 5 MINS   ❄ **FREEZE** UP TO 3 MONTHS

1 large onion, chopped
2 tbsp olive oil
10oz–1lb 2oz (300–500g) shoulder
   of lamb on the bone
1 tsp ground ginger
1 tsp ground cinnamon
leaves of 1 small bunch parsley,
   finely chopped
leaves of 1 small bunch cilantro,
   finely chopped

5½oz (150g) brown lentils, rinsed
1 x 14oz (400g) can chopped tomatoes
2 tbsp tomato purée
salt and freshly ground black pepper
3½oz (100g) vermicelli noodles
1 x 14oz (400g) can chickpeas, drained, or
   14oz (400g) cooked chickpeas
3 tbsp flour
lemon wedges, to serve

1 Cook the onion gently in the oil until translucent. While it cooks, cut the meat from the lamb bones in 1¼in (3cm) cubes. Reserve the bones.

2 Once the onions are tender, stir in the ginger, cinnamon, half the parsley, and half the cilantro, then add the lamb chunks and bone and turn to coat evenly. Now add the lentils, tomatoes, and tomato purée and season with salt and freshly ground black pepper. Mix well and simmer for a few minutes, then add 1¾ quarts (1¾ liters) of water. Let simmer for 45 minutes, then remove the lamb bones and add the vermicelli and chickpeas.

3 Put the flour in a small bowl with a ladleful of the cooking liquid and stir to make a smooth paste the consistency of thick cream, adding more liquid if needed. Stir this back into the soup and simmer for another 3–4 minutes until it has thickened and the vermicelli is cooked.

4 Just before serving, stir in the remaining herbs, and adjust the seasoning. Serve with wedges of lemon.

This vegetable and lentil dish is best served piping hot, in cavernous bowls. You can find pink lentils (*masoor dal*) in most Asian food stores.

kichidi

⊘ SERVES 6–8   **⏱ PREP** 15 MINS **COOK** 50 MINS   **❄ FREEZE** UP TO 3 MONTHS
AT THE END OF STEP 3

1 butternut squash, about 1lb 9oz (700g)
½ tsp garam masala
salt and pepper
2 tbsp olive oil
3½oz (100g) basmati rice
3½oz (100g) pink or red lentils
2in (5cm) ginger, peeled and finely grated

2 tbsp ghee or clarified butter
2 tsp cumin seeds
½ tsp crushed hot red pepper flakes
juice of 1 lime
3 tbsp chopped cilantro
2 tbsp unsalted butter

1   Preheat the oven to 400°F (200°C). Halve the squash lengthwise and scoop out the seeds and fibers. Put it in a roasting pan, cut side up, sprinkle with the garam masala, season with salt and pepper, and drizzle with the oil. Cover with foil and roast for 45 minutes, or until meltingly tender. Let cool slightly, then scoop out the flesh, lightly crush it with a fork, and set aside.

2   Meanwhile, combine the rice and lentils in a large saucepan and cover with 2 quarts (2 liters) of water. Add the ginger, bring to a boil, then reduce the heat and simmer for about 30 minutes until the rice grains have lost their texture and broken down. Add more hot water to loosen the texture, if desired. Stir in the lightly crushed squash.

3   Heat the ghee in a separate pan and cook the cumin and red pepper flakes for about 30 seconds, until aromatic and darker in color. Tip the spices and ghee into the rice and lentils and stir well, seasoning with plenty more salt and pepper.

4   Stir in the lime juice and cilantro. Divide between deep bowls and finish with a generous dollop of butter in the center of each helping.

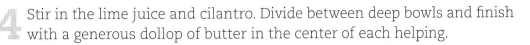

The chicken drumstick makes this a questionable dish for your vegetarian friends—unless you don't mind stretching the truth. It can, of course, be left out.

chickpea soup

SERVES 6   **PREP** 15 MINS, PLUS OVERNIGHT SOAKING   **FREEZE** UP TO 3 MONTHS
COOK 1 HR 40 MINS

7oz (200g) chickpeas, soaked in water
  overnight, then drained
2.5 quarts (2.5 liters) cold water
1 chicken drumstick
4 tbsp olive oil
2 celery ribs, chopped
1 medium onion, chopped

1 medium leek, chopped
3 garlic cloves, finely sliced
salt and freshly ground black pepper
½ cup dry white wine
1 tbsp lemon juice
6 tbsp extra virgin olive oil, to serve
2 tbsp chopped chives and parsley, to garnish

1 Place the chickpeas in a saucepan with plenty of cold water and bring to a boil. Skim away any foam with a slotted spoon, then drain and return to the pan. Add the cold water and chicken, bring to a boil, and skim again. Cover with a lid and simmer for 1½ hours or until the peas are done. Lift out the chicken after 45 minutes, remove the meat, and set to one side.

2 Heat 1 tbsp of the oil in a frying pan, add the celery, onion, and leek, and cook for 5–10 minutes or until soft. Add the garlic, season with salt and freshly ground black pepper, then cook for another minute. Add the contents of the frying pan to the chickpeas, then stir in the cooked chicken. Pour in a little water if the mixture seems too thick to blend.

3 Transfer the soup to a blender and process in batches until smooth, adding the wine, lemon juice, and the remaining 3 tbsp olive oil in three or four stages. Season with salt and freshly ground black pepper, then return to the pan and heat through. Divide the soup among six bowls, float 1 tbsp of extra virgin olive oil on the top of each one, then serve garnished with the chopped chives and parsley.

If chervil isn't available, you can replace it with a few leaves of fresh mint to finish. You can also use frozen peas if fresh peas are out of season.

potage saint germain

SERVES 4   **PREP** 15 MINS **COOK** 1 HR   **FREEZE** UP TO 3 MONTHS
BEFORE MADEIRA IS ADDED

1 tbsp sunflower, peanut, or
  mild-flavored olive oil
1 tbsp butter plus 2 tbsp chilled
  butter, diced
4 large scallions (white parts only), chopped
1½ quarts (1½ liters) hot chicken or
  vegetable stock
5½oz (150g) split green peas, rinsed
  and drained

sea salt and freshly ground black pepper
1lb 2oz (500g) fresh green peas
  (about 1¾lb/800g unshelled)
1 small head soft lettuce, leaves snipped
1 large egg yolk
3 tbsp crème fraîche
1–2 tbsp Madeira or port
few sprigs of chervil

1 Put a large sauté pan over medium heat. Add the oil and 1 tbsp butter, then stir in the scallions. Reduce the heat a little and cook for 5 minutes, stirring frequently. Pour the hot stock into the pan, and then add the split peas. Season lightly with salt and pepper, and bring back to a simmer. Reduce the heat, cover, and cook for another 20 minutes, stirring occasionally.

2 Add the garden peas and the lettuce, stir, and cook for 5 minutes. Let cool a little, then pour the contents of the pan into a blender or food processor and process until smooth. Push the soup back into the pan through a fine sieve, mashing the vegetables with the back of a spoon to extract as much as possible. Pour ½ cup water through the sieve to thin down the soup. Reheat gently over low heat.

3 In a cup or small bowl combine the egg yolk and the crème fraîche with 2–3 tablespoons of the hot soup. Whisk this into the pan a little at a time. Continue cooking until the soup is piping hot. Adjust the seasoning. Just before serving, stir in the Madeira or port. Whisk in the diced butter and sprinkle a little snipped chervil over the top.

Be careful when seasoning this hearty soup, as the bacon means that little, if any, extra salt will be needed. Try this soup with olive oil croûtons.

split pea and bacon soup

SERVES 6   **PREP** 30 MINS **COOK** 1 HR 10 MINS   **FREEZE** UP TO 3 MONTHS

9oz (250g) dried split green peas, rinsed and drained
1½ quarts (1½ liters) water
4–5 slices thick-cut bacon
¼ celeriac, peeled and diced
1 large carrot, diced
1 small leek, diced

1 medium floury potato, peeled and diced
1 tsp dried marjoram
1 tbsp butter
1 onion, diced
freshly ground black pepper
3–4 tsp chopped chives, to garnish

1 Put the peas in a large saucepan with the water and bring to a boil. Add the bacon, cover, and cook for about 40 minutes over medium heat. Add the celeriac, carrot, leek, and potato, and stir in the marjoram. Bring to a boil again, cover, and cook for another 20 minutes.

2 Melt the butter in a separate pan, and add the onion. Brown slightly, stirring continuously, then set aside.

3 Remove the bacon from the soup, chop, and return it to the soup together with the cooked onion. Season with pepper. Sprinkle with chopped chives to serve.

As delicate as it is delicious, this pretty, pastel-green soup is scented with citrusy cardamom notes, which make a marvelous marriage with the pounded pistachios.

creamy pistachio soup

◎ SERVES 2–3 　 **◐ PREP** 40 MINS **COOK** 20 MINS 　 **❄ FREEZE** UP TO 3 MONTHS
WITHOUT HALF-AND-HALF
AND CILANTRO

4½oz (125g) (shelled weight) unsalted
　pistachio nuts
1 green chile, cut in half and seeded
½ cup hot water
6 green cardamom pods, crushed and
　seeds extracted
1 small blade of mace
½ tsp coriander seeds, dry-roasted (see p25)
2 tbsp butter
2 large garlic cloves, finely chopped

small bunch of scallions (white parts only),
　finely chopped
1in (2.5cm) piece of ginger, peeled
　and finely chopped
½ tsp garam masala
2 cups hot vegetable stock
3½fl oz (100ml) half-and-half
1 tbsp chopped cilantro
salt and freshly ground black pepper

1 Bring a pan of water to a boil, add the pistachios, and cook for about 2–3 minutes. Drain in a colander and refresh under cold running water. Pat the nuts dry with paper towels, then turn out on to a kitchen towel. Give them a vigorous rub with the towel—the skins should slip off easily. Reserve a generous tablespoon for garnishing and put the rest in a food processor. Add the chile and hot water and process to a rough paste, then set aside.

2 Grind the cardamom seeds, mace, and coriander to a powder with a pestle and mortar. Melt the butter in a saucepan over medium heat, add the garlic, scallions, and ginger, and soften for 2–3 minutes. Stir in the ground spices and garam masala and cook for a few seconds, then add the pistachio paste and stock. Simmer without a lid for 10–15 minutes, stirring occasionally.

3 Blend in batches until smooth. Stir in the cream and cilantro, then season with salt and freshly ground black pepper. Serve the soup garnished with the reserved pistachio nuts coarsely chopped.

This Spanish soup is seriously garlicky, but heavenly in summer. You could reduce the number of garlic cloves to as few as two—if you wish.

white gazpacho

SERVES 4   **PREP** 20 MINS   **FREEZE** NOT SUITABLE

3oz (85g) white bread (crusts removed),
   cut into cubes
2 cups ice water
9oz (250g) whole blanched almonds
6 garlic cloves, coarsely chopped

3 tbsp olive oil
3 tbsp sherry vinegar or white
   balsamic vinegar
salt and freshly ground black pepper
5½oz (150g) seedless white grapes

1 Soak the bread in all but 3 tbsp of the ice water for 10 minutes. Meanwhile, place the almonds in a food processor and process until ground as finely as possible. Add the remaining 3 tbsp ice water and blend to a paste. Remove the bread from the water (reserving the water) and add to the processor, along with the garlic, and blend again.

2 With the motor running, gradually add the water the bread soaked in, followed by the oil. Keep pulsing until the mixture is absolutely smooth. Add the vinegar and season to taste with salt and freshly ground black pepper. To serve, place a handful of grapes in the bottom of each bowl, ladle the soup on top, then drizzle with a little olive oil, if desired.

fish and shellfish

Originally nothing more than a humble fisherman's soup using the remains of the day's catch, bouillabaisse has evolved into one of the great Provençal dishes.

bouillabaisse

SERVES 4   **PREP** 20 MINS **COOK** 45 MINS   ❋ **FREEZE** NOT SUITABLE

4 tbsp olive oil
1 onion, thinly sliced
2 leeks, thinly sliced
1 small fennel bulb, thinly sliced
2–3 garlic cloves, finely chopped
4 tomatoes, peeled, seeded, and chopped
1 tbsp tomato purée
1 cup dry white wine
1½ quarts (1½ liters) fish or chicken stock
pinch of saffron threads
strip of orange zest
1 bouquet garni
salt and freshly ground black pepper
2 tbsp Pernod

3lb (1.35kg) mixed white and oily fish and shellfish, such as monkfish, red mullet, shrimp, and mussels, heads and bones removed
8 croûtes, to serve

for the rouille
4¼oz (125g) mayonnaise
1 bird's-eye chile, seeded and coarsely chopped
4 garlic cloves, coarsely chopped
1 tbsp tomato purée
½ tsp salt

1 Heat the oil in a large pan over medium heat. Add the onion, leeks, fennel, and garlic and cook, stirring, for 5–8 minutes, or until the vegetables are soft but not colored. Stir in the tomatoes, purée, and wine.

2 Add the stock, saffron, zest, and bouquet garni. Season with salt and pepper, and bring to a boil. Reduce the heat, partially cover, and simmer for 30 minutes, stirring occasionally. Process the rouille ingredients in a blender until smooth. Transfer to a bowl, cover, and chill until required.

3 Just before the liquid finishes simmering, cut the fish into chunks. Remove the zest and bouquet garni and add the firm fish. Reduce the heat to low and simmer for 5 minutes. Add the delicate fish and simmer for 2–3 minutes, or until it is cooked through and flakes easily. Stir in the Pernod and season to taste. To serve, spread the croûtes with rouille and place 2 in the bottom of each bowl. Ladle the soup on top.

The seafood must be just-cooked, so cut dense fish in small pieces or add it earlier. Try red mullet, bass, haddock, cod, salmon, turbot, raw shrimp, or scallops.

north sea fish soup

⊘ SERVES 4   **⏱ PREP TIME** 20 MINS **COOK** 20 MINS   **❄ FREEZE** NOT SUITABLE

1lb 2oz (500g) mixed fish fillets and shellfish
salt and frehly ground black pepper
1 tbsp lemon juice
2½ cups fish or chicken stock
¼ cup white wine
2 shallots, chopped

1 egg yolk
1 tbsp heavy cream
1 tomato, peeled, seeded, and chopped
1 tbsp chopped parsley
croûtons, to serve

1 Skin the fish, if necessary, and cut into 1in (2.5cm) pieces. Season and add the lemon juice. Bring the stock, white wine, and shallots to a boil in a large saucepan.

2 Add the fish in the order it takes to cook depending on which you are using: red mullet or bass first, 2 minutes later the turbot, if using, followed by any haddock, cod, or salmon and, finally, shrimp or scallops. Simmer uncovered until all the fish is just cooked.

3 Stir the egg yolk and cream together in a bowl. Remove the soup from the heat, stir in the egg mixture, then add the tomato and parsley. Serve with croûtons.

This soup was originally a way to use the leftover catch of the day in Brittany. Try it with haddock, smoked haddock, pollock, or cod.

cotriade (fish stew)

SERVES 4　　**PREP** 20 MINS **COOK** 30 MINS　　**FREEZE** NOT SUITABLE

2 large floury potatoes, peeled
2 tbsp peanut, sunflower, or mild olive oil
2 tbsp butter
2 Spanish onions, coarsely chopped
1 quart (1 liter) light fish stock
3 sprigs of thyme
3 bay leaves
3 sprigs of flat-leaf parsley
sea salt and freshly ground black pepper
1¾lb (800g) mixed fish, skinned and cut into
　large chunks
4 thick slices country bread, to serve

for the dressing
5–6 tbsp peanut, sunflower, or mild olive oil
½ tsp Dijon mustard
sea salt and freshly ground black pepper
1 tbsp white wine or cider vinegar
2 tbsp finely chopped parsley

1 Cut the potatoes into quarters and set aside. Heat the oil and butter in a large, heavy sauté pan over medium heat. Add the onions and soften until just golden, stirring frequently. Add the stock, then add in the potatoes and herbs. Season lightly with salt and pepper, stir, cover, and cook for 12–15 minutes or until the potatoes are almost cooked.

2 Place the fish in the pan and season lightly. Gently stir, then cook for 7–10 minutes, or until the fish just starts to flake when pierced with a fork. If you are freezing the soup, cool and do so now. Meanwhile, make the dressing. In a small bowl, mix together the oil and mustard. Season with salt and pepper, then whisk in the vinegar until emulsified. Stir in the parsley.

3 Remove the soup from the heat and adjust the seasoning. Remove the herbs. Put the bread in 4 warm bowls and moisten with a little dressing. Ladle the soup over the top and drizzle on the remaining dressing. Serve hot.

This flavorful soup needs no accompaniment, but croûtes rubbed with garlic, spread with rouille (see p234), or topped with Gruyère cheese are a welcome addition.

soupe de poissons

SERVES 6　　**PREP** 20 MINS **COOK** 1 HOUR　　**FREEZE** UP TO 2 MONTHS

5 tbsp olive oil
4 medium onions, chopped
2 leeks, chopped
3lb 3oz–4½lb (1½–2kg) mixed fish
　and seafood
4 pieces dried fennel stalks, 2in (5cm) long
4 medium, ripe tomatoes, quartered
9 garlic cloves, crushed

5 sprigs of fresh flat-leaf parsley
3 bay leaves
6in (15cm) strip dried orange peel
1 tbsp tomato purée
salt and freshly ground black pepper
pinch of saffron threads
6 croûtes, to serve

1 Put the oil in a large, heavy saucepan. Add the onions and leeks and soften over medium heat until just golden.

2 Gut the larger fish, and rinse all the fish and seafood. Add to the pan and stir, then add the fennel, tomatoes, garlic, parsley, bay leaves, orange peel, and tomato purée. Stir and cook for 8–10 minutes until the fish is just beginning to flake when pierced with a fork. Pour in 2½ quarts (2½ liters) hot water and season lightly with salt and pepper. Reduce the heat and simmer gently for 20 minutes.

3 Remove from the heat. Let cool a little, stirring and mashing down the soft fish pieces with the back of a large wooden spoon. Remove the fennel, orange peel, and bay leaves. If you like, process the soup to a coarse purée in a blender. Push the soup through a chinois or a very fine sieve into a clean saucepan. Return the soup to a simmer over medium heat.

4 Soften the saffron in a ladleful of the soup, then stir into the rest of the soup in the pan. Adjust the seasoning. Ladle the soup into bowls. Serve hot, with croûtes.

This rustic, Mediterranean-style fish soup—robustly flavored with brandy, orange, and fennel—is simple to prepare and sure to please.

fish soup with fennel

SERVES 4–6   **PREP** 10 MINS **COOK** 1 HR   ✳ **FREEZE** NOT SUITABLE

2 tbsp butter
3 tbsp olive oil
1 large fennel bulb, finely chopped
2 garlic cloves, crushed
1 small leek, sliced
4 ripe plum tomatoes, chopped
3 tbsp brandy
¼ tsp saffron threads, infused in a little hot water
zest of ½ orange
1 bay leaf

1¾ quarts (1¾ liters) fish stock
10oz (300g) potatoes, diced and parboiled for 5 minutes
4 tbsp dry white wine
1lb 2oz (500g) fresh black mussels, scrubbed and debearded
salt and freshly ground black pepper
1lb 2oz (500g) monkfish or other firm white fish, cut into bite-sized pieces
6 raw whole tiger prawns
parsley, chopped, to garnish

1 Heat the butter with 2 tbsp of the oil in a large, deep pan. Stir in the fennel, garlic, and leek, and cook over medium heat, stirring occasionally, for 5 minutes, or until softened and lightly browned.

2 Stir in the tomatoes, add the brandy, and boil rapidly for 2 minutes, or until the juices are reduced slightly. Stir in the saffron, orange zest, bay leaf, fish stock, and potatoes. Bring to a boil, then reduce the heat and skim off any foam from the surface. Cover and simmer for 20 minutes, or until the potatoes are tender. Remove the bay leaf.

3 Meanwhile, heat the remaining oil with the wine in a large, deep pan until boiling. Add the mussels, cover, and continue on high heat for 2–3 minutes, shaking the pan often. Discard any mussels that do not open. Strain, reserving the liquid, and set the mussels aside. Add the liquid to the soup and season to taste. Bring to a boil, add the monkfish and prawns, then reduce the heat, cover, and simmer gently for 5 minutes, or until the fish is just cooked and the prawns are pink. Add the mussels to the pan and bring almost to a boil. Serve the soup sprinkled with chopped parsley.

A German soup, from the region of Schleswig-Holstein on the North Sea coast. You can use any white fish, so choose whatever is freshest.

büsumer fish soup

⊘ **SERVES** 6–8   🕐 **PREP** 15 MINS **COOK** 20 MINS   ❄ **FREEZE** NOT SUITABLE

2 large carrots, chopped
1 large potato peeled and diced
1 large onion, diced
1 quart (1 liter) hot vegetable stock
1 bay leaf
salt and freshly ground black pepper
1lb 2oz (500g) white fish fillets, such as
   haddock, cleaned and cubed

juice of 1 lemon
7oz (200g) button or cremini
   mushrooms, sliced
3½oz (100g) raw peeled jumbo shrimp
½ cup heavy cream
½ bunch of dill, chopped

1 Put the carrots, potato, and onion into a saucepan, add the hot stock and bay leaf, and bring to a boil. Reduce the heat and simmer for 10 minutes.

2 Sprinkle a little salt and pepper and half the lemon juice over the fish pieces, then add these to the stock along with the mushrooms and simmer for another 5 minutes over low heat.

3 Add the shrimp to the pan along with the remaining lemon juice, and cook for 3 minutes, or until they turn pink. Remove the bay leaf and season with salt and pepper, to taste. Stir in the cream and half the dill and serve immediately, using the remaining dill to garnish.

If you enjoy the intense salty-sweetness of eel, you'll love this German-style soup. Contact your fishmonger in advance to order a fresh eel, asking for it to be prepared.

hamburg eel soup

SERVES 6   **PREP** 15 MINS **COOK** 1 HR 20 MINS   **FREEZE** UP TO 2 MONTHS

3¼ cups Riesling wine
2 tbsp white wine vinegar
2 tbsp chopped fresh parsley
1 onion, sliced
2 carrots, diced
1 bay leaf
salt and freshly ground black pepper

1 prepared eel (cleaned, skinned, and cut
  into 2in/5cm pieces)
2 tbsp butter
1½ tbsp flour
2 quarts (2 liters) hot vegetable stock
bouquet garni (see p24)

1 Pour the wine and 2 cups of water into a large saucepan with the vinegar, then add the chopped parsley, onion, carrots, and bay leaf, and season with salt and pepper. Bring to a boil and cook for 4–6 minutes. Add the eel pieces and simmer over low heat for 10 minutes, or until the flesh is tender, then let cool.

2 Melt the butter in a saucepan, add the flour, and cook until blended. Stir in the stock a little at a time. Add the bouquet garni to the pan, and cook slowly for 1 hour.

3 To serve, remove the eel pieces from the cooking liquid. Stir half the cooking liquid into the vegetable stock, divide the eel pieces between six bowls, and ladle the soup over.

Henningsvaer is a picturesque little port town in Norway's Lofoten Islands, and this soup is the speciality of a small restaurant there.

henningsvaer fish soup

SERVES 6-8   **PREP** 15 MINS **COOK** 45 MINS   **FREEZE** NOT SUITABLE

1½ quarts (1½ liters) fish stock
12oz (350g) cod fillet
4 tbsp butter
1 onion, finely chopped
1 large carrot, finely chopped
1 large leek, finely chopped

2 tsp sugar
2 tbsp white wine vinegar
salt and freshly ground black pepper
1¼ cups crème fraîche
chopped parsley, to serve

1 Bring the stock to a boil. Add the cod, bring gently back to a boil, then remove from the heat. When cool enough to handle, lift out the cod and flake, discarding skin and stray bones. Set aside the fish and stock.

2 Melt the butter in a large pan and add the vegetables. Stir to coat, then cover the pan, reduce the heat to very low, and let cook for 20 minutes, stirring once or twice. Add the stock, sugar, and vinegar, season with salt and pepper, and bring to a boil. Simmer for 10 minutes. Stir in the crème fraîche and flaked fish. Taste and adjust the seasoning, then reheat gently without boiling. Serve immediately, sprinkled with the parsley.

Replace the mussels with shell-on shrimp in this Flemish soup if you prefer; peel, and add the empty shells to the reduced stock for 3 minutes before straining.

waterzooi (flemish stew)

SERVES 4 **PREP** 20 MINS **COOK** 30 MINS **FREEZE** NOT SUITABLE

1 large waxy potato, peeled
1 large carrot, peeled
1 medium-large zucchini
1 bunch asparagus
10oz (300g) monkfish
1 sole, filleted and skinned
2½ cups chicken or fish stock

½ cup dry white wine
3 large scallions, finely chopped
1lb 2oz (500g) mussels, rinsed and scrubbed
½ cup heavy (whipping) cream
salt and freshly ground black pepper
1 tbsp finely chopped tarragon, to serve

1 Cut the potato and carrot in ½ x 2in (1 x 5cm) batons. Slice the zucchini into diagonal pieces. Cut off the asparagus tips, then chop the spears into 2in (5cm) lengths. Cut the monkfish into 1½in (4cm) chunks and cut each sole fillet crosswise in half. Set the vegetables and fish aside separately.

2 Place the stock, wine, and scallions (reserving a few to serve) in a heavy saucepan. Bring to a boil over medium heat. Add the potato, reduce the heat to a simmer, and cook for 5 minutes, then add the carrot and cook for 5 minutes. Add the zucchini and asparagus and cook for 1–2 minutes, or until all is *al dente*. Remove the vegetables and set aside.

3 Bring the stock to a boil over high heat and reduce by a third. Reduce the heat to a simmer, add in the mussels, cover and cook for 3–4 minutes. Strain through a muslin-lined sieve into a bowl, let cool briefly, then discard any mussels that haven't opened. Shell the rest and set aside. Return the stock to the pan and simmer over medium heat, then stir in the cream and season to taste with salt and pepper. Add the monkfish, cook for 2–3 minutes, then the sole for 1 minute, then the vegetables and mussels for a final 2 minutes.

4 Using a slotted spoon, distribute the vegetables between the bowls. Place the fish on top, ladle over the broth, and scatter with mussels. Sprinkle with chopped tarragon and the reserved scallion. Serve hot.

This is a complete meal in a bowl. Raw mangoes add bite to a citrusy broth flecked with fiery red chiles. Raw mangoes are available in many Asian markets.

mango and snapper broth

SERVES 4   **PREP** 15 MINS, PLUS 20 MINS MARINATING   **FREEZE** NOT SUITABLE   **COOK** 15 MINS

1 tbsp soy sauce
2 tsp Asian fish sauce
1 tbsp toasted sesame oil
1 tbsp mirin
1 tsp sugar
juice of 1 lime
1lb (500g) skinless red snapper fillets, cut into 1in (2.5cm) cubes
2 stalks lemongrass, finely chopped
2 tbsp vegetable oil
4 bird's eye red chiles, finely sliced
4 scallions, finely sliced
2in (5cm) fresh ginger, finely shredded
4 garlic cloves, coarsely chopped

4 small raw green mangoes, or under-ripe mangoes, peeled and finely chopped
2 tsp palm sugar or brown sugar
2 tbsp rice wine vinegar
1 quart (1 liter) fish stock
8 kaffir lime leaves, torn in half
1 tbsp Asian fish sauce
4oz (100g) medium egg noodles
4oz (100g) thin green beans, halved
salt to season
juice of 1 lime, to taste
2 tbsp chopped fresh cilantro leaves
1 tbsp shredded fresh mint leaves

1 Combine the soy and fish sauce, sesame oil, mirin, sugar, and lime juice, and spoon over the fish. Refrigerate for 20 minutes. Pound the lemongrass to a paste with a dash of water, using a mortar and pestle. Set aside.

2 Heat the oil in a wok or large pan and cook the chiles, scallions, ginger, and garlic for 30 seconds over high heat. Add the mangoes and cook for 1 minute. Stir in the sugar until it begins to caramelize. Add the vinegar, lemongrass, stock, lime leaves, and fish sauce. Bring to a boil.

3 Stir in the noodles, beans, and fish pieces (not the marinating liquid). Simmer for 3–5 minutes, until the noodles are cooked and the fish flakes easily. Season with salt, sharpen with lime juice, and add the herbs.

The strong flavors of cavolo nero and smoked haddock develop in minutes, making this soup very satisfying. If you want to freeze it, do so before adding the fish.

portuguese haddock soup

SERVES 4　　**PREP** 20 MINS **COOK** 20 MINS　　　**FREEZE** NOT SUITABLE

10oz (300g) leaves of cavolo nero, kale, or savoy cabbage
2 tbsp olive oil
1 Spanish onion, finely chopped
3 garlic cloves, peeled and crushed

1 large waxy potato, peeled and diced
1 cup milk
salt and freshly ground black pepper
10oz (300g) smoked haddock fillet, skinned and flaked

1 Rinse the greens, cut out and discard the large ribs, and shred the leaves finely. Set aside. Place a heavy saucepan over medium heat and add the oil. Once it is hot, add the onion and garlic and cook for 4–5 minutes, or until softened.

2 Add the potato and milk, then pour in enough water to cover everything by ¾–1¼in (2–3cm). Season, bring to a simmer, and cook for 5 minutes, then add the greens and continue cooking for 10–15 minutes until the vegetables are tender.

3 Stir in the haddock and simmer for 1 minute, then take off the heat and cover. Let stand for 5 minutes before serving.

This comforting soup is based on a simple roux-based sauce, so it is vital to use very good stock to make it really sing. It makes an excellent light lunch.

creamy smoked trout soup

SERVES 6   **PREP** 15 MINS **COOK** 10 MINS   **FREEZE** UP TO 2 MONTHS

3½ tbsp butter
¼ cup flour
3¼ cups hot vegetable or fish stock
1 cup heavy (whipping) cream
4 tbsp white wine
2–3 tsp Worcestershire sauce

salt and freshly ground black pepper
squeeze of lemon juice
13oz (375g) smoked trout fillets,
  skinned and flaked
2 tbsp chopped parsley

1 Over low heat, melt the butter in a large saucepan, stir in the flour, and mix until smooth. Cook for 2–3 minutes, stirring constantly. Gradually pour in the hot stock, making sure there are no lumps by whisking vigorously. Bring to a boil and then cook, uncovered, over low heat for about 3 minutes, stirring occasionally.

2 Add the cream, white wine, Worcestershire sauce, salt, pepper, and a little lemon juice, then bring to a boil again. Add the fish pieces and briefly heat them through. Sprinkle the soup with parsley and serve.

TROUT
Be sure to buy smoked trout for this dish, as it is already cooked. Go for whole moist fillets, because some pre-flaked fish can be dry. Always keep yourself informed of fish sustainability guidelines.

Make sure you don't boil the soup after adding the miso paste, as it spoils the flavor. You'll find wakame (dried seaweed) and miso in large supermarkets.

miso soup with tuna

⦿ **SERVES** 4   🕐 **PREP** 25 MINS **COOK** 15 MINS   ❄ **FREEZE** NOT SUITABLE

4in (10cm) piece wakame
2 tbsp dried shiitake mushrooms
2 scallions, chopped
1 tsp grated fresh ginger
1 long thin carrot, thinly sliced

2 cups chicken stock
7oz (200g) fresh tuna steak, diced
2 tbsp miso paste
soy sauce, to season
1 tbsp snipped chives

1 Put the wakame and mushrooms in a bowl and cover with cold water. Soak for 15 minutes. Drain, reserving the liquid. Lift out the wakame, remove any hard central ribs, and cut into strips.

2 Put the wakame, mushrooms, scallions, ginger, and carrot into a saucepan. Combine 1¼ cups of the soaking water with the stock and add to the saucepan. Bring to a boil, reduce the heat, cover, and simmer for 10 minutes until the carrot is just tender.

3 Add the tuna and cook for another 5 minutes. In a small bowl, blend the miso paste with 2 tbsp water and stir in to the soup. Season to taste with soy sauce. Heat through but do not boil. Ladle into warm soup cups and sprinkle with snipped chives.

A rich main meal soup naturally thickened with okra—
a classic gumbo ingredient. In its native Louisiana, sweet
ground sassafras leaves would be used.

mixed seafood gumbo

SERVES 6   **PREP** 20 MINS **COOK** 50 MINS   ❄ **FREEZE** UP TO 2 MONTHS
AT THE END OF STEP 2

1 tbsp sunflower oil
1 onion, chopped
2 celery ribs, chopped
1 large garlic clove, chopped
4oz (115g) chorizo, sliced
2 tbsp plain flour
2½ cups fish or chicken stock
1 x 14oz (400g) can chopped tomatoes
1 green bell pepper, diced

9oz (250g) okra, trimmed and cut
  into short lengths
¼ tsp cayenne pepper
½ tsp dried oregano
½ tsp sugar
salt and freshly ground black pepper
7oz (200g) mixed raw seafood
8oz (225g) long-grain rice
chopped parsley, to serve

1 Heat the oil in a large saucepan. Add the onion and celery and cook gently, stirring, for about 5 minutes, or until lightly golden. Stir in the garlic and chorizo and cook for 2 minutes. Stir in the flour and cook for another minute. Remove from the heat and gradually blend in the stock, then the tomatoes. Return to the heat and bring to a boil, stirring. Add the remaining ingredients, except the seafood and rice, bring back to a boil, reduce the heat, partially cover, and simmer gently for 30 minutes.

2 Add the seafood and simmer for another 5 minutes, stirring from time to time. Taste and season again to taste.

3 Meanwhile, cook the rice in plenty of boiling, lightly salted water for 10 minutes or until just tender (or as the package directs). Drain in a colander, rinse with boiling water, and drain again.

4 Spoon some rice into each of 6 large soup bowls. Ladle the gumbo over the top, sprinkle with a little chopped parsley, and serve hot.

in praise of...
shellfish
There are few greater pleasures than gathering mussels at low tide, and then feasting on these delicious fruits of the sea.

A delicious fall soup for the whole family. Purée it for the younger members, so they get to eat their required vegetables without noticing.

potato and clam soup

◎ SERVES 4–6   **◷ PREP** 25 MINS **COOK** 1 HR 30 MINS   **❄ FREEZE** NOT SUITABLE

2¼lb (1kg) clams
¼ cup dry white wine
2–3 tbsp olive oil
2 celery ribs, finely diced
1 red onion, finely chopped
1 carrot, finely chopped
4 tomatoes, peeled, seeded, and chopped

2 medium potatoes, finely diced
1 quart (1 liter) cold water
1 sprig of rosemary
1 tbsp finely chopped flat-leaf parsley
  or chervil
salt and freshly ground black pepper
4–6 slices thick country bread

1 Wash the clams thoroughly in cold running water, throwing away any with broken shells and any that are open and won't close when gently tapped. Put them in a large frying pan with the wine, cover with a lid, and place over high heat for 5 minutes or until the shells open. Discard any that remain closed, as they will not be edible. Drain, reserving the liquid. Remove the clams from their shells, place in a bowl, cover, and refrigerate until needed. Strain the cooking liquid through a fine sieve.

2 Heat the oil in a large heavy-bottomed pan, add the celery, onion, and carrot, and cook on low heat for 10 minutes or until light brown. Add the tomatoes, potatoes, the reserved cooking liquid, and the water, and bring to a boil. Add the rosemary, then lower the heat, cover with a lid, and simmer for 1 hour.

3 Stir in the clams and the parsley or chervil, then season with salt and freshly ground black pepper. Remove the rosemary, put a slice of bread in the bottom of each bowl, and ladle over the soup.

This traditional, creamy soup is often served with oyster crackers, although crusty bread is also good. The clams must be cooked on the day of purchase.

new england clam chowder

🍽 **SERVES** 4   🕐 **PREP** 15 MINS **COOK** 35 MINS   ❄ **FREEZE** NOT SUITABLE

36 live clams
1 tbsp oil
4oz (115g) thick-cut bacon, diced
2 floury potatoes, such as russet, peeled and
   cut into ½in (1cm) cubes
1 onion, finely chopped

2 tbsp flour
2½ cups whole milk
salt and freshly ground black pepper
½ cup half-and-half
2 tbsp finely chopped flat-leaf parsley

1 Discard any open clams, then shuck the rest, reserving the juices. Add enough water to the juices to make 2½ cups. Chop the clams. Heat the oil in a large, heavy saucepan and cook the bacon over medium heat for 5 minutes or until crisp. Remove and drain on paper towels.

2 Add the potatoes and onion to the pan and cook for 5 minutes or until the onion has softened. Add the flour and stir for 2 minutes. Stir in the clam juice and milk and season to taste. Cover with a lid, lower the heat, and simmer for 20 minutes or until the potatoes are tender. Add the clams and simmer gently, uncovered, for 5 minutes. Stir in the half-and-half and reheat without boiling. Serve sprinkled with the bacon and parsley.

SHUCKING CLAMS

Work the tip of a knife between the top and bottom shell, then twist upward to open the clam.

Sever the muscle at the top, then do the same at the bottom to release the clam meat.

There are several variations on Manhattan clam chowder, using vegetables such as celery and green bell peppers. Its defining feature, however, is its tomato base.

manhattan clam chowder

SERVES 4   **PREP** 15 MINS **COOK** 35 MINS   ✳ **FREEZE** NOT SUITABLE

36 live clams, freshly bought
1 tbsp oil
3–4 slices thick-cut bacon, diced
1 onion, finely chopped
2 floury potatoes, such as russet, peeled
and cut into ½ in (1cm) cubes

2 tbsp flour
2 x 14oz (400g) cans chopped tomatoes
with their juice
salt and freshly ground black pepper
fresh thyme, to garnish

1 Discard any clams that are open. Shuck the clams and reserve the juice, adding enough water to make 2½ cups. Chop the clams.

2 Heat the oil in a large, heavy saucepan and cook the bacon over medium heat, stirring frequently, for 5 minutes, or until it is crisp. Remove from the pan with a slotted spoon, drain on paper towels, and set aside.

3 Add the onion and potatoes to the pan and cook for 5 minutes, or until the onion has softened. Add the flour and stir for 2 minutes.

4 Stir in the tomatoes and their juice and season to taste with salt and pepper. Cover the pan, reduce the heat, and let simmer for 20 minutes or until the potatoes are tender. Add the clams and simmer gently, uncovered, for 5 minutes. Serve the chowder hot, sprinkled with bacon and thyme.

This is a wonderful, unusual, inspired soup. The combination of saffron and curry powder gives it an interesting aromatic quality.

mussel and saffron soup

SERVES 4   **PREP TIME** 15 MINS **COOK** 35 MINS   **FREEZE** NOT SUITABLE

½ cup dry white wine
2 cups fish or chicken stock
4½lb (2kg) mussels, scrubbed
   and debearded
2 tbsp butter
4½oz (125g) onions, finely chopped
2 carrots, diced
3oz (85g) celeriac, diced

1 thin leek, finely sliced
1 garlic clove, chopped
1½ tsp curry powder
good pinch of saffron threads,
   soaked in 2 tbsp hot water
1 cup heavy cream
salt and pepper
2 tbsp parsley, finely chopped

1 Bring the wine and stock to a boil in a large deep pan over high heat. Add the mussels, discarding any that will not shut when tapped, and cover. As the mussels open, remove them to a bowl. When all are open, filter the liquid through muslin into another bowl. Discard two-thirds of the shells.

2 Clean the pan. Melt the butter over low heat and add the vegetables and garlic, stirring well. Cook gently for 10 minutes, then stir in the curry powder and add the mussel liquid and the saffron in its water. Add the cream and cook without boiling for 5 minutes. Return the mussels to the pan, heat through gently, and season well. Sprinkle over the parsley, and serve.

SCRUBBING AND DE-BEARDING MUSSELS

Scrub the mussels under cold running water, then scrape off any barnacles with a knife.

Pinch the dark stringy "beard" between forefinger and thumb and pull it firmly away.

These succulent mussels in their moat of gingery juices are terrific with a mound of fluffy rice on the side, but crusty bread mops up the broth just as nicely.

mussels in a ginger and chile broth

SERVES 2–4   **PREP** 20 MINS **COOK** 30–35 MINS   **FREEZE** NOT SUITABLE

3lb (1.5 kg) mussels, in their shells, cleaned
1 stick (8 tbsp) butter
2 onions, finely chopped
2 bird's-eye red chiles, finely chopped
2in (5cm) fresh ginger, finely shredded
5 large garlic cloves, finely chopped
2 stalks lemongrass, split lengthwise
    and lightly bruised

½ cup ginger liqueur
1¾ cups fish stock
⅔ cup coconut milk
3 tbsp coconut cream
salt and freshly ground black pepper
juice of 1–2 limes, to taste
3 tbsp chopped fresh cilantro

1 Wash the mussels under cold running water. Give any open ones a firm tap against the counter top and discard any that don't close.

2 Melt the butter in a large pan over low heat and soften the onions, chiles, ginger, garlic, and lemongrass for 10 minutes without coloring.

3 Turn the heat up to high and add the ginger liqueur followed by the stock. Bring to a boil before adding the mussels. Cover the pan and cook for 5–7 minutes, until the mussel shells have opened. Discard the lemongrass along with any mussels that remain closed.

4 Pour in the coconut milk and cream, and bring to a boil. Season with salt and pepper, sharpen with lime juice, stir in the cilantro, and serve.

A wonderfully elegant soup that marks the crossover between foods that are coming into season and those that are going out of season.

soup of the first and last

⊘ **SERVES** 4–6   🕐 **PREP** 30 MINS **COOK** 45 MINS   ✳ **FREEZE** NOT SUITABLE

10 oysters, opened, and with juice
1 tbsp butter
1 white onion, finely diced
2 garlic cloves, finely chopped
1 celery rib, finely diced
salt and freshly ground black pepper
¾ cup heavy cream
1¾ cups cold water
½ celeriac, peeled and finely diced

7oz (200g) russet potatoes, cut into thin slices
2 small–medium turnips, cut in two, then sliced into half-moons
7oz (200g) garlic leaves, cut into roughly 1¾in (4cm) pieces (or substitute baby spinach and extra garlic)
a handful of wild garlic flowers, to garnish (optional)

1 Wash 4–6 oyster shells (one per serving) to remove any grit. Cover with boiling water, to clean and keep warm. Heat the butter in a pan, add the onion, garlic, celery, and a pinch of salt, cover with a lid, and cook over low heat for 5 minutes or until soft. Add the cream, water, and celeriac and simmer, covered, for 10 minutes. Add the potatoes and cook for 10 minutes, then add the turnips and cook for 10 more minutes.

2 Take off the heat and ladle half the soup into a blender. Add 4–6 oysters (depending on how many you need to serve) and half the garlic leaves and blend until smooth. Tip the mixture back in the pan, rinse the blender out with 1¾ cups cold water, and add that to the pan as well. Season with salt and freshly ground black pepper, add the rest of the garlic leaves, then bring to a gentle simmer and cook for 5 minutes.

3 Meanwhile, put the remaining oysters and their juices in a pan with 2 tbsp water, and poach for 4 minutes or until firm. Turn halfway through. Stir the juice (but not the oysters) into the soup, then check the seasoning and the consistency—add a little hot water if the soup is too thick. Divide among 4–6 bowls. Drop a warm oyster shell in each, fill with a poached oyster, and garnish with wild garlic flowers if desired.

The name 'bisque' refers to a rich and luxurious shellfish soup with cream and brandy and is thought to have come from the Spanish Biscay region.

lobster bisque

SERVES 4   **PREP** 45 MINS **COOK** 1 HR 10 MINS   **FREEZE** UP TO 3 MONTHS

1 lobster, cooked, about 2¼lb (1kg) in weight
3½ tbsp butter
1 onion, finely chopped
1 carrot, finely chopped
2 celery ribs, finely chopped
1 leek, finely chopped
½ fennel bulb, finely chopped
1 bay leaf
1 sprig of tarragon
2 garlic cloves, crushed

2½oz (75g) tomato purée
4 tomatoes, coarsely chopped
½ cup Cognac or brandy
½ cup dry white wine or vermouth
1¾ quarts (1¾ liters) fish stock
½ cup heavy cream
salt and freshly ground black pepper
pinch of cayenne
juice of ½ lemon
chives, to garnish

1 Split the lobster in half, remove the meat from the body, and chop the meat into small pieces. Twist off the claws and legs, break at the joints, and remove the meat, then crack all the shells with the back of a knife. Chop the shells into coarse pieces and put the meat into the refrigerator.

2 Melt the butter in a large pan over medium heat, add the vegetables, herbs, and garlic, and cook for 10 minutes, or until softened, stirring occasionally. Add the lobster shells. Stir in the tomato purée, tomatoes, Cognac, white wine, and fish stock. Bring to a boil and simmer for 1 hour.

3 Let cool slightly, then ladle into a food processor. Process in short bursts, until the shell breaks into very small pieces. Strain through a coarse sieve, pushing through as much as you can, then pass it again through a fine sieve before returning to the heat.

4 Bring to a boil, add the reserved lobster meat and the cream, then season to taste, adding the cayenne and lemon. Serve in warm bowls, garnished with chives.

This fragrant soup takes the best ingredients from a cottage garden in the southern Indian state of Kerala. If you are using dried curry leaves, add them with the stock.

keralan shrimp soup

SERVES 4–6   **PREP** 20 MINS **COOK** 40 MINS   **FREEZE** NOT SUITABLE

1 tsp black peppercorns
¾ tsp mustard seeds
2 tsp coriander seeds
½ tsp fenugreek seeds
2–3 large red chiles, coarsely chopped
4 garlic cloves, chopped
2in (5cm) piece fresh ginger, chopped
4 tbsp hot water
2–3 tbsp vegetable oil

small handful of fresh curry leaves
2 onions, finely chopped
3¼ cups fish stock
1 cup coconut milk
9oz (250g) raw jumbo shrimp, shelled
1 tbsp coconut cream
2 tbsp fresh cilantro, chopped
juice of 1 lime, to taste

1 Heat a sturdy frying pan over low heat. Roast the peppercorns, mustard, coriander, and fenugreek seeds for about 30 seconds, until they give off a spicy aroma and the mustard seeds start to pop. Grind the spices to a powder using a mortar and pestle, and set aside.

2 Put the chiles in a small food processor with the garlic and ginger. (If you like a milder flavor, use just 2 chiles and remove the seeds.) Pour in the hot water and process to a paste. Set aside.

3 Heat the oil in a wok or saucepan. When hot, toss in the curry leaves and cook for 20 seconds, Be careful; curry leaves spit when added to hot oil. Add the onions, cover, and soften for 10 minutes, stirring occasionally.

4 Stir in the chile, garlic, and ginger paste and cook for 2–3 minutes, until the water evaporates. Add the ground spice mixture and cook for another 30 seconds, stirring all the time. Pour in the stock and simmer for 20 minutes or until reduced by one-third. Stir in the coconut milk and reheat before adding the shrimp and cooking for another 4–5 minutes. Add the coconut cream and finish with the cilantro and enough lime juice to sharpen.

poultry, game, and meat

A universal favorite, this soup has a zingy parsley and lemon finish. It can also be made with leftover meat and the carcass of a roasted chicken.

traditional chicken soup

◉ SERVES 4   **◕ PREP** 2½ HRS **COOK** 30 MINS   **✳ FREEZE** UP TO 3 MONTHS
BEFORE HALF-AND-HALF IS ADDED

for the stock
1 small to medium free-range chicken
1 large carrot, chopped
1 leek, cut into segments
3 garlic cloves, unpeeled
¾oz (20g) dried mushrooms
3 celery ribs, chopped
2–3 sprigs each of parsley and thyme
sea salt and freshly ground black pepper

for the soup
3½oz (100g) short grain rice or pearl barley
1½ tbsp vegetable oil plus 10g (¼oz) butter
½ large red onion, finely chopped
2 garlic cloves, crushed
9oz (250g) button mushrooms, thinly sliced
4 tbsp half-and-half
2 tbsp finely chopped parsley
2 tsp finely grated zest of an unwaxed lemon

1 For the stock, place the chicken in a large saucepan over low heat. Cover with water and bring slowly to a boil, skimming the surface as needed. Add the carrot, leek, garlic, dried mushrooms, celery, and herbs. Season lightly. Bring back to a simmer, partially cover, and cook for 1 hour.

2 Remove from the heat. Once cool, lift out the chicken, strip the meat from the carcass, and reserve. Return the carcass to the pan and boil for 1 hour. Let cool, strain through a sieve into a bowl, and chill the stock.

3 Soak the rice or barley in cold water for 30 minutes. Rinse and drain. Skim the fat from the chilled stock. You'll need 3¼ cups of stock for the soup recipe, but you can add boiling water if needed.

4 Put the oil and butter in a deep saucepan over medium heat. Add the vegetables and cook for 3–5 minutes. Add the rice or barley, and stir for 2 minutes. Add the stock and cook for 15–20 minutes. Shred about 7oz (200g) of the reserved chicken and add to the soup. Taste, season if necessary, and return to a simmer. Stir in the half-and-half, parsley, and lemon zest, and serve very hot.

The traditional method involves slow-simmering a whole chicken, but this version takes less time and effort. To make a more substantial meal, add a few boiled potatoes.

cock-a-leekie soup

SERVES 4   **PREP** 10 MINS **COOK** 1¼ HRS   ❄ **FREEZE** UP TO 3 MONTHS

1lb (450g) chicken breasts
  and thighs, skinned
2 bay leaves
1 quart (1 liter) chicken or
  vegetable stock
2oz (60g) long-grain rice

2 leeks, thinly sliced
2 carrots, grated
pinch of ground cloves
1 tsp sea salt
1 tbsp chopped fresh parsley

1 Place the chicken in a large pan with the bay leaves and pour in the stock. Bring to a boil, then reduce the heat, cover the pan, and simmer for 30 minutes.

2 Skim the surface of the soup and discard any foam that has formed. Add the rice, leeks, carrots, cloves, and salt. Bring back to a boil, reduce the heat, cover the pan, and simmer for another 30 minutes.

3 Remove the bay leaves and discard. Lift out the chicken, remove the meat from the bones, then return the meat to the soup. Ladle the soup into a warm tureen or divide between individual serving bowls, and serve hot, garnished with parsley.

CHICKEN
Free-range chickens are afforded space to move around in and access to the open air, making them healthier than caged birds, and this is reflected in the taste. Choose a bird with a firm, plump breast and tight skin.

This Mexican soup is made with thin *fideo* noodles, which are similar to angel-hair pasta. The avocado and sour cream offset the spiciness of the broth.

sopa seca de fideos

SERVES 4   **PREP** 20 MINS PLUS 30 MINS SOAKING **COOK** 15 MINS   **FREEZE** NOT SUITABLE

2 dried chipotle chiles
2 large ripe tomatoes, peeled and seeded
2 garlic cloves
1 small onion, coarsely chopped
1 quart (1 liter) chicken stock
3 tbsp vegetable oil

2 skinless boneless chicken breasts, diced
8oz (225g) Mexican *fideo* noodles or dried angel-hair pasta
4 tbsp sour cream, to serve
1 avocado, pit removed, chopped, to serve

1 Soak the dried chiles in water for 30 minutes, then drain, discarding the soaking water. Using a blender, process the tomatoes, garlic, onion, chiles, and 2 tbsp of the stock until smooth. Set aside.

2 Heat 2 tbsp of the oil in a large pan over medium heat and stir-fry the chicken for 2–3 minutes, or until just cooked. Remove from the pan, drain on paper towels, and set aside.

3 Pour the remaining oil into the pan, add the noodles, and cook over low heat, stirring constantly, until the noodles are golden.

4 Pour in the tomato mixture, stir until the noodles are coated, then add the remaining stock and return the chicken to the pan. Cook for 2–3 minutes, or until the noodles are just tender. To serve, ladle into bowls, topping each with sour cream and chopped avocado.

Here, a nourishing chicken stock combines with the sweetness of sweet corn and satisfying vermicelli to create a soothing meal in a bowl.

chinese chicken noodle soup

⊘ **SERVES** 4   🕐 **PREP** 10 MINS PLUS 30 MINS SOAKING   ❄ **FREEZE** NOT SUITABLE
                         COOK 15 MINS

1½oz (45g) dried Chinese mushrooms
2½ cups chicken stock
2 skinless boneless chicken breasts

6oz (175g) dried rice vermicelli
3½oz (100g) sweet corn kernels

1 Place the dried Chinese mushrooms in a heatproof bowl, pour in 1¼ cups boiling water, and let stand for 30 minutes. Reserving the mushrooms, strain the soaking water into a large saucepan and add the stock. Bring the pan to a boil.

2 Slice the mushrooms and cut the chicken breasts into bite-sized pieces or thin strips. Break the rice vermicelli into short lengths and stir into the pan. Bring to a simmer and cook for 2 minutes.

3 Add the mushrooms, chicken, and sweet corn kernels to the pan, bring back to a boil, and simmer for another 2 minutes, or until the vermicelli is tender. Spoon into bowls and serve at once.

The pasta and the liberal quantities of vegetables ensure that this chicken soup goes a long way. You can use whatever fresh vegetables are available.

chicken soup with pasta

SERVES 4–6   **PREP** 10 MINS **COOK** 1 HR   **FREEZE** UP TO 3 MONTHS

4 chicken drumsticks
2¾lb (1.25kg) mixed vegetables, e.g., carrots (diced), kohlrabi (diced), green beans (ends trimmed and strings removed), cauliflower or broccoli (small florets), leeks (sliced), zucchini (sliced), peas

3½oz (100g) vermicelli pasta
sea salt and freshly ground black pepper
2 tablespoons chopped parsley

1 Place the chicken drumsticks in a large saucepan, cover with 1¼ quarts (1¼ liters) cold water, and bring to a boil. Cover and cook over medium heat, skimming occasionally with a slotted spoon, for about 40 minutes. Remove from the heat and strain into a clean pan, then allow the stock to cool slightly before skimming the fat from the surface with a spoon.

2 Remove and discard the skin from the chicken drumsticks, strip the meat from the bones, shred, and reserve.

3 Bring the stock back to a boil, then add the vegetables. Add those with longer cooking times first, cover, and simmer for 5 minutes; then add the remaining vegetables and the vermicelli, cover, and cook for another 5 minutes.

4 Season the soup with salt and pepper to taste. Add the reserved meat and heat it through. Ladle into bowls, garnish each with a little chopped parsley, and serve piping hot.

Based on a Thuringian vegetable soup, this recipe requires a good-quality, well-flavored chicken stock, so make your own for best results.

german chicken broth

SERVES 4-6   **PREP** 10 MINS **COOK** 25 MINS   ❄ **FREEZE** UP TO MONTHS
AT THE END OF STEP 1

1¼ quarts (1¼ liters) chicken stock
5oz (150g) green beans, ends trimmed
  and strings removed
2 large carrots, peeled and sliced
7oz (200g) kohlrabi, diced

5½oz (150g) sugar snap peas, ends trimmed
salt and freshly ground black pepper
heavy cream, to serve
1 bunch chervil, finely chopped

1 Bring the stock to a boil in a medium-sized saucepan, add the green beans, and simmer for 5 minutes. Add the carrots and kohlrabi and cook for another 5 minutes, then add the sugar snap peas and cook for 5 minutes more—be careful not to overcook these or they will lose their delightful crunchiness.

2 Season with salt and pepper and remove the pan from the heat. Ladle into serving bowls, add a swirl of cream to each, and sprinkle with chervil before serving.

SUGAR SNAP PEAS
These are most often steamed, lightly boiled, or stir-fried, but they can also be enjoyed raw. The fresher the produce, the better the flavor and texture, so make sure you go for firm, smooth, bright green pods.

This is a traditional soup with a modern twist. Adding baking powder and mashed potato to the balls gives them a really light, fluffy texture.

matzo ball soup

SERVES 4   **PREP** 15 MINS **COOK** 1 HR 10 MINS   **FREEZE** UP TO 3 MONTHS
BROTH ONLY

1 chicken leg and thigh portion
1 onion, finely chopped
1 leek, thinly sliced
1 large carrot, finely diced
1 quart (1 liter) water
1 sprig of fresh thyme
1 tsp celery salt
salt and freshly ground black pepper

for the matzo balls
1 potato, about 4oz (115g), cooked
   and mashed

1½oz (45g) fine matzo meal
½ tsp baking powder
½ tsp grated fresh ginger
1 tbsp chopped fresh thyme
1 tbsp chopped fresh parsley
1 garlic clove, finely chopped
salt and freshly ground black pepper
1 tbsp sunflower oil
1 egg, beaten
4 small sprigs of fresh thyme, to garnish

1 Put the soup ingredients in a large saucepan. Bring to a boil, reduce the heat, cover, and simmer gently for 1 hour, adding more water if it gets low. Meanwhile, mix the mashed potatoes with the matzo meal, baking powder, ginger, thyme, parsley, garlic, and a little salt and pepper. Add the oil, then mix with the beaten egg to form a soft, slightly sticky dough. Shape into 8 balls.

2 Discard the thyme sprig from the soup. Carefully lift out the chicken and remove all meat from the bones, discarding the skin. Chop the meat and return to the soup. Taste and adjust the seasoning, if necessary.

3 Bring the soup back to a simmer, drop in the balls, cover, and simmer gently for about 10 minutes until fluffy and cooked through. Ladle into warm soup bowls and garnish each with a small sprig of fresh thyme.

Consommé regularly has some garnish or herb to lend interest, but it is the quality and clarity of the soup itself that is at its heart.

chicken consommé

SERVES 4　　**PREP TIME** 15 MINS PLUS CHILLING　　**FREEZE** NOT SUITABLE
COOK 1 HR 20 MINS

2 large egg whites
1 tbsp passata or 1 tsp tomato purée
1 chicken leg, boned and minced or
　finely chopped
1 onion, chopped
1 carrot, chopped

1 leek, chopped
1 garlic clove, chopped
1 tbsp chopped parsley
2 quarts (2 liters) cold chicken stock
salt and freshly ground pepper
chervil, to garnish

1 To make the clarification mixture, whisk the egg whites just enough to loosen them and form a few bubbles. Add the passata or tomato purée and mix thoroughly.

2 Place the chicken, vegetables, garlic, and parsley in a bowl, add the egg white mixture, and mix thoroughly—use an electric mixer with paddle attachment if need be. Refrigerate until well chilled.

3 Combine the stock with the clarification mixture in a deep, narrow saucepan. Heat slowly, uncovered, until the stock comes to a boil. Gently stir to keep the egg from sticking. Once the stock reaches boiling point, turn the heat down immediately and let simmer gently for at least an hour, or until a white crust forms. When it is hard, poke a hole through it to check on the clarity.

4 When the consommé is clear and the clarification ingredients cooked, widen the hole and strain the consommé through a muslin-lined sieve into a clean container. Season with salt and pepper, garnish with chervil, and serve.

This can be a simple chicken broth with just the drizzled egg, but it's more tasty and filling with the addition of vegetables and Chinese seasonings.

chinese egg drop soup

SERVES 4   **PREP** 5 MINS **COOK** 25 MINS   **FREEZE** NOT SUITABLE

1 quart (1 liter) chicken stock
1 garlic clove, crushed
½ tsp grated fresh ginger
2 scallions, chopped
2 tbsp soy sauce
½ tsp Chinese five-spice powder

2 corn on the cob or 1 x 7oz (200g) can sweet corn
2 good handfuls of fresh baby leaf spinach
2 tbsp cornstarch
2 eggs, beaten

1 Put the stock in a pan with the garlic, ginger, scallions, soy sauce, and five-spice powder. If using fresh corn, place each corn on the cob on its end and slide a sharp knife down the length to remove all the kernels. Add the kernels to the pan, bring to a boil, reduce the heat, cover, and simmer gently for 20 minutes.

2 Add the canned sweet corn if using, including any liquid, and the spinach. Bring back to a boil, reduce the heat, and simmer for 1 minute or until the spinach has just wilted. Taste and add more soy sauce if necessary.

3 Blend the cornstarch with 4 tbsp water and stir in. Bring back to a boil and simmer, stirring, for 1 minute to thicken slightly. Gradually trickle in the beaten egg, stirring gently, so that it forms thin strands. Serve in warm soup bowls.

This lemon, chicken, and rice soup is claimed by countries across the eastern Mediterranean. The stock must be well flavored, or it will not withstand the lemon juice.

avgolemone

⊘ SERVES 4   **⏱ PREP** 5 MINS **COOK** 20 MINS   **❄ FREEZE** NOT SUITABLE

¼ cup long-grain rice
1¼ quarts (1¼ liters) well-flavored
  chicken stock
3 eggs

juice of 1 large lemon
salt and freshly ground black pepper
lemon wedges, to serve

1 Bring the rice and stock to a boil in a saucepan. Simmer, uncovered, for 15 minutes, or until the rice is completely cooked.

2 Whisk the eggs and lemon juice in a bowl until the mixture becomes frothy. Add a ladleful of hot stock and continue to whisk.

3 Remove the rice and stock from direct heat. Whisk the egg, lemon, and stock mixture into it. Return to the heat and cook gently and briefly at a temperature below boiling point, whisking until the texture is velvety—do not allow to boil. Season with salt and pepper and serve with lemon wedges.

Although this recipe uses coconut milk as its base and key Thai flavorings, it makes no pretense of authenticity. No extra salt should be necessary, as *nam pla* is salty.

thai chicken soup

SERVES 4   **PREP** 10 MINS **COOK** 45 MINS   **FREEZE** NOT SUITABLE

4 stalks lemongrass, bruised and cut
  into ½in (1cm) lengths
7oz (200g) galangal, peeled and diced
5 kaffir lime leaves, bruised
1 chicken leg
2 cups water

2 small red chiles
1 litre (1¾ pints) coconut milk
1 tbsp *nam pla* or Asian fish sauce
juice of 3 limes
3 scallions, finely chopped
2 tbsp chopped cilantro

1 Put the lemongrass, galangal, lime leaves, chicken, and water in a pan and bring to a boil. Simmer uncovered for 30 minutes, or until the chicken is cooked. Remove with a slotted spoon, dice the flesh, discarding the skin and bones, and set aside.

2 Add the chiles to the pan and bring the soup back to a boil. Pour in the coconut milk and heat slowly—you want the soup to become hot enough for the flavors to infuse the coconut milk without coming to a boil.

3 Strain the soup into a clean pan or tureen. Remove the chiles from the sieve and cut into slivers. Add the *nam pla*, lime juice, scallions, cilantro, and chicken to the soup, then taste to check the seasoning. Serve garnished with the chile slivers.

CHILES
Look for fresh, bright, shiny-looking chiles, and avoid any that have soft patches or look wrinkled. Wrapped in a biodegradable plastic bag, they will keep in the crisper drawer of the refrigerator for up to 2 weeks.

Chicken, honey, and herb sausages are used in this hearty soup, but it is also excellent made with any other tasty pure-meat sausages or chorizo.

sausage and bean soup

SERVES 4   **PREP** 20 MINS **COOK** 30–35 MINS   **FREEZE** UP TO 3 MONTHS

9oz (250g) cherry tomatoes, halved
4 tbsp olive oil, plus extra to serve
salt and freshly ground black pepper
1 onion, finely chopped
7oz (200g) organic chicken or other good-quality pure-meat sausages or chorizo, peeled and roughly crumbled
4 garlic cloves, finely chopped

½–1 tsp crushed hot red pepper flakes (according to taste)
1 x 14oz (400g) can cannellini beans, drained, rinsed, and drained again
about 3 cups hot chicken stock or vegetable stock
1 tbsp balsamic vinegar
1 handful flat-leaf parsley or basil, chopped

1 Preheat the oven to 350°F (180°C). Place the tomatoes on a baking sheet, drizzle with half the oil, sprinkle with a couple of pinches each of salt and freshly ground black pepper, then turn to coat well. Roast for about 15 minutes or until softened and slightly wilted, then remove from the oven and drizzle with the balsamic vinegar.

2 Meanwhile, heat the remaining oil in a heavy-bottomed pot over medium heat. Add the onion and cook for 5 minutes or until soft. Stir in the sausagemeat, garlic, and hot red pepper flakes, and cook, stirring, for 5–10 minutes or until the onion is pale yellow. Stir in the beans and stock, bring to a boil, adjust the heat to a steady simmer and cook for 10 minutes. Add the tomatoes and their juices and stir in half the parsley or basil.

3 Ladle out a cupful of the beans and tomatoes without too much liquid, and process until smooth in a blender. Stir back into the pot, then simmer the soup steadily for 10 minutes. If it is too thick, thin with a little hot stock or water. Stir in the rest of the herbs and adjust the seasoning, adding salt, freshly ground black pepper, pepper flakes, and balsamic vinegar to taste. Ladle into warmed bowls, drizzle with a little more olive oil, and serve.

You can vary this dish by substituting smoked pork sausage for pancetta or using duck instead of chicken. You may wish to add a little filé powder, if you have it.

chicken and pork gumbo

SERVES 6   **PREP** 20 MINS **COOK** 1½ HRS   ❄ **FREEZE** UP TO 3 MONTHS
WITHOUT THE RICE

2 chicken leg and thigh portions
7oz (200g) diced pancetta
2 boneless belly pork slices, rinded and diced
1 quart (1 liter) chicken stock
1 bay leaf
2 red bell peppers
2 tbsp butter
1 onion, chopped
1 garlic clove, chopped
1 celery rib, sliced
3 tbsp flour
2 beefsteak tomatoes, peeled and chopped

2 tbsp tomato purée
4oz (115g) thin green beans, trimmed
   and cut in short lengths
5½oz (150g) okra, cut in short lengths
2 large sprigs of fresh thyme, chopped,
   plus a little extra to garnish
2 tsp sweet paprika
1 tsp smoked paprika
1 tsp brown sugar
a few drops of Tabasco
salt and freshly ground black pepper
8oz (225g) long-grain rice, cooked

1 Put the chicken, pancetta, and pork slices in a saucepan with the stock and bay leaf. Bring to a boil, reduce the heat, cover, and simmer gently for 1 hour. Meanwhile, roast the peppers under a broiler for 10–15 minutes until blackened. Put in a plastic bag, let cool, then peel off the skin, discard the stalks and seeds, rinse, and dice the flesh.

2 Strain the stock through a sieve and set aside. Lift the chicken out of the sieve and place on a board. Remove all the meat from the bones and cut into small pieces, discarding the skin. Add to the pork and set aside.

3 Melt the butter in the pan. Cook the onion, garlic, and celery for 2 minutes, stirring. Stir in the flour and cook for 3 minutes, stirring, until golden. Remove from the heat and blend in the stock. Return to the heat and bring to a boil. Add the remaining ingredients except the meat and rice. Bring back to a boil, reduce the heat, partially cover, and simmer for 30 minutes. Stir in the meats, taste and season with Tabasco, salt, and pepper. Remove the bay leaf. Spoon the rice into bowls, ladle the gumbo over, and garnish with thyme.

An Anglo-Indian soup from colonial days, mulligatawny has many variations. For extra heat, pop a split red chile in the pan when you add in the stock.

mulligatawny

⊘ **SERVES** 4　　🕐 **PREP** 20 MINS **COOK** 45 MINS　　❄ **FREEZE** UP TO 3 MONTHS

2½ tbsp butter
1 large onion, chopped
2in (5cm) fresh ginger, finely chopped
2 garlic cloves, finely chopped
1 apple, diced with peel
1 carrot, sliced
1 celery rib, sliced
1 heaped tbsp mild curry powder
1 tbsp flour

4 tomatoes, coarsely chopped
2 tsp tomato purée
2 cups hot chicken stock
2 bay leaves
salt and freshly ground black pepper
¾ cup coconut milk or half-and-half
7oz (200g) cooked chicken meat, shredded
2 tbsp chopped fresh cilantro
juice of ½ lime

1　Melt the butter in a large pan and soften the onion, ginger, and garlic for 10 minutes, without coloring. Add the apple, carrot, and celery to the pan and continue cooking, covered, for 5 minutes.

2　Stir in the curry powder and cook for 1 minute, stirring all the time. Sprinkle in the flour and continue cooking for another 20 seconds.

3　Add the tomatoes and tomato purée followed by the chicken stock. Add the bay leaves and season with salt and pepper. Bring to a boil, stirring, then reduce the heat and simmer, half-covered, for 20 minutes.

4　Remove the bay leaf and blend until smooth, using a stick blender or liquidizer. Sieve the soup to remove any fibers and skin. Reheat, stir in the coconut milk or half-and-half, and add the diced chicken. Sharpen with a squeeze of lime and add the chopped cilantro.

Make good use of leftover turkey by simmering your own stock with the carcass after a roast dinner. This broth is every bit as appealing when made with chicken.

turkey broth

SERVES 6   **PREP** 20 MINS **COOK** 25 MINS   **FREEZE** UP TO 3 MONTHS
BEFORE CREAM IS ADDED

1 quart (1 liter) turkey stock or
   chicken stock
½ cup dry white wine
1 carrot, finely diced
1 parsnip, finely diced
2 celery ribs, finely diced
1 leek (white part only), finely diced

1 small turnip, finely diced
salt and freshly ground black pepper
8oz (225g) cooked turkey meat, finely diced
½ cup half-and-half
2 tbsp chopped parsley
crusty bread, to serve

1 Bring the stock and wine to a boil in a large pan, then stir in the carrot, parsnip, celery, leek, and turnip. Season with salt and freshly ground black pepper, half-cover with a lid, and simmer for 20 minutes.

2 Stir in the cooked turkey, cream, and chopped parsley and reheat gently. Serve the soup with plenty of crusty bread.

This is a substantial soup that is a great way to make one partridge feed four people. You could use any other small game bird in exactly the same way.

partridge soup

SERVES 4   **PREP** 20 MINS **COOK** 1 HR 5 MINS   **FREEZE** UP TO 3 MONTHS
WITHOUT THE SHERRY

1 tbsp sunflower oil
1 partridge, quartered
1 onion, unpeeled and quartered
1 quart (1 liter) chicken stock
1 bouquet garni
salt and freshly ground black pepper
1 potato, diced
1 carrot, diced

1 small turnip, diced
2 tbsp plain flour
4 tbsp water
7oz (200g) cooked peeled
　chestnuts, quartered
2 tbsp amontillado sherry
a few drops of soy sauce
a little chopped fresh parsley

1 Heat the oil in a saucepan and brown the partridge pieces all over. Add the onion, stock, bouquet garni, and a little salt and pepper. Bring to a boil, reduce the heat, cover, and simmer gently for 1 hour.

2 Strain the stock and return to the saucepan. Add the potato, carrot, and turnip. Bring back to a boil, partially cover, and simmer gently for about 20 minutes until the vegetables are really tender. Meanwhile, take all the meat off the partridge, discarding the skin, and shred the meat.

3 Remove the bouquet garni from the soup and discard. Blend the flour with the water and add to the soup. Bring to a boil, stirring, until lightly thickened, and simmer for 2 minutes.

4 Add the shredded meat, chestnuts, and sherry to the soup and simmer for 2 minutes. Add a few drops of soy sauce to taste. Ladle into warm soup bowls and garnish with a little chopped parsley.

You can buy ready-diced mixed game which includes furred game and pigeon, or use diced venison, rabbit, or hare. Aged beef is another option.

puff-crusted game soup

🔘 **SERVES** 4　　🕐 **PREP** 20 MINS **COOK** 1 HR 20 MINS　　❄️ **FREEZE** UP TO 3 MONTHS
AT THE END OF STEP 2

1–2 tbsp butter
6oz (175g) diced game meat, thawed
　if frozen, cut into small pieces
1 red onion, chopped
2 tbsp plain flour
1 quart (1 liter) beef stock
1 tbsp redcurrant jelly

3 button mushrooms, halved and sliced
1 tbsp chopped fresh sage
4 tbsp ruby port
salt and freshly ground black pepper
1 sheet ready-rolled puff pastry,
　thawed if frozen
1 egg, beaten

1　Melt the butter in a saucepan and cook the meat and onion for 5 minutes, stirring, until browned.

2　Blend in the flour and cook for 1 minute. Remove from the heat, gradually stir in the stock, add the jelly, and bring to a boil, stirring. Add the mushrooms, sage, port, and some seasoning. Bring back to a boil, reduce the heat, cover, and simmer very gently for 1 hour, stirring from time to time until rich and really tender. Taste and adjust the seasoning if necessary.

3　Meanwhile, preheat the oven to 425°F (220°C). Cut four circles from the pastry slightly larger than deep oven-proof soup cups and brush with beaten egg. Stand the soup cups on a baking sheet. Brush the edges with beaten egg. Ladle in the soup. Top with the circles of pastry, pressing down lightly with a fork around the edge to secure. Make a small slit in the top of each pie lid with a sharp knife to allow the steam to escape. Bake in the oven for about 15 minutes or until puffy, crisp, and golden brown. Allow to cool for 3–5 minutes before serving.

This classic French soup takes time to make, but is well worth waiting for. Try serving this with coarse-grained mustard, gherkins, and creamed horseradish.

pot au feu

⊙ **SERVES** 4   🕐 **PREP** 40 MINS **COOK** 2 HRS   ❄ **FREEZE** NOT SUITABLE

a few beef bones, if possible

2¼lb (1 kg) braising steak cut into 2–2½in (5–6cm) pieces

salt and freshly ground black pepper

1 large carrot, thickly cut on the diagonal

2 turnips, thickly sliced

1 medium-to-large waxy potato, cut into 8 pieces

1 Spanish onion, halved

2 garlic cloves, crushed

3 cloves

1 large leek, thickly sliced

3 celery ribs, chopped

3 bay leaves

several sprigs each of thyme and parsley

1 Put any bones in a large, deep, heavy pan. Place the meat on top of the bones. Cover with plenty of cold water, at least 2½in (6cm) above the meat, and very slowly bring to a simmer over low heat. Season lightly with salt and pepper. Skim off any foam that rises to the surface. Cover and let simmer very gently for 1 hour, while you prepare the vegetables. Cut one half of the onion into slices and press the cloves into the other half.

2 Skim the meat again. Add the prepared vegetables to the pan, with the bay leaves, thyme, and parsley. Bring back to a simmer and skim again. Season lightly. Reduce the heat, partially cover, and cook gently for at least 45 minutes, until the meat and vegetables are tender.

3 Skim again if necessary, then lift out the meat and vegetables and put in a large shallow bowl or in individual bowls. Discard the bones, the onion stuck with cloves, bay leaves, thyme, and parsley.

4 Strain the stock into a saucepan through a muslin-lined sieve. Bring to a simmer and season if required. Ladle sufficient stock over the meat and vegetables. Let the remaining stock cool. There should be plenty left for you to use in other dishes (keep refrigerated for up to 3 days, or freeze).

Warming and hearty, this soup is great served with tortilla chips and some guacamole (avocado mashed with lime juice) on hand to spoon in.

beef chili

SERVES 4   **PREP** 10 MINS **COOK** 35 MINS   ❄ **FREEZE** UP TO 3 MONTHS

1 tbsp olive oil
1 onion, chopped
8oz (225g) lean ground beef
½ tsp crushed dried chiles
1–2 fresh red chiles, seeded and chopped
1 tsp ground cumin
1 tsp dried oregano
2 cups passata

2 cups beef stock
1 x 14oz (400g) can red kidney beans,
   drained and rinsed
1 tbsp tomato purée
½ tsp sugar
salt and freshly ground black pepper
1 tbsp chopped fresh cilantro or parsley
grated Manchego or Cheddar cheese, to serve

1 Heat the olive oil in a large saucepan, add the onion, and cook for 4–5 minutes or until softened but not colored. Add the beef and cook, stirring, until the grains of meat are separated and no longer pink.

2 Stir in the dried and fresh chiles and cumin and cook for 30 seconds, stirring. Add the oregano, passata, stock, red kidney beans, tomato purée, sugar, and salt and pepper. Bring to a boil, stirring. Reduce the heat, partially cover, and simmer gently for 30 minutes, stirring occasionally. Taste and adjust the seasoning if necessary.

3 Ladle into warm soup bowls and sprinkle with the cilantro or parsley. Serve topped with grated Manchego or Cheddar cheese.

The warming flavors of steak and onions make this soup a rich and satisfying meal. For an authentic touch, use Hungarian paprika—it is fairly readily available these days.

hungarian goulash soup

SERVES 6–8   **PREP** 15 MINS **COOK** 2 HRS   **FREEZE** UP TO 3 MONTHS

4 tbsp olive oil
1½lb (675g) onions, thinly sliced
2 garlic cloves, crushed
1½lb (675g) chuck steak, cut into
    2in (5cm) cubes
salt and freshly ground black pepper

2 tbsp paprika
1 tsp caraway seeds
1 tsp cayenne pepper, plus extra to garnish
4 tbsp tomato purée
1 quart (1 liter) beef stock
sour cream, to garnish

1 Heat 3 tbsp of the olive oil in a large heavy saucepan over medium heat, add the onions, and cook, stirring occasionally, for 10 minutes or until they are golden brown. Add the garlic for the final 2 minutes, then remove from the heat.

2 Heat the remaining oil in a frying pan, add the steak, and cook, stirring often, for 5 minutes or until brown on all sides. Season with salt and add to the onions, along with the spices and tomato purée. Return the saucepan to the heat and cook for 5 minutes, stirring all the time, then pour in the stock. Cover with a lid and simmer gently for 1¾ hours.

3 Season to taste with salt and freshly ground black pepper, then serve the soup garnished with sour cream, a sprinkling of cayenne, and some more freshly ground black pepper.

Choose firm, waxy potatoes that will keep their shape and texture in this deliciously savory soup. Cooking the beans until just *al dente* retains maximum taste and color.

beef and green bean soup

SERVES 6   **PREP** 20 MINS **COOK** 1 HR   ❄ **FREEZE** UP TO 3 MONTHS

2 tbsp sunflower oil
1lb 2oz (500g) braising beef (from the
   shoulder), diced into ¾in (2cm) cubes
salt and freshly ground black pepper
1 onion, chopped
2–3 sprigs of thyme

1 quart (1 liter) vegetable stock
1 large potato, cut into chunks
9oz (250g) fresh green beans, trimmed and
   cut into small pieces
1–2 tbsp chopped fresh parsley (optional)

1 Heat the oil in a pan, season the cubed meat with salt and pepper, and add half the meat to the hot oil. Brown the meat until golden all over. Remove from the pan and repeat with the the next batch. When finished, remove all the meat from the pan, add the onion, and cook until softened.

2 Transfer the browned meat back to the pan, tie the thyme sprigs together with kitchen string, and add them to the pan with the stock. Bring to a boil, cover, and cook over medium heat for about 40 minutes.

3 Add the potato, bring back to a boil, cover, and cook for 10–15 minutes, or until just tender. Add the chopped beans and cook for 4–5 minutes, or until the beans are *al dente*.

4 Remove the thyme. Season to taste with salt and pepper, break up the meat pieces slightly, and sprinkle with parsley, if using, before serving.

Enriched with sherry, this slow-cooked soup is a classic for flavorful comfort eating. If you prefer a chunky texture, the soup also tastes good unblended.

oxtail soup

◉ SERVES 6   **◷ PREP** 20 MINS, PLUS 1 HR CHILLING
COOK 4 HRS 45 MINS

❄ FREEZE UP TO 3 MONTHS
WITHOUT THE SHERRY

2 tbsp vegetable oil
salt and freshly ground black pepper
1lb 5oz (600g) oxtails, disjointed, available
   from your butcher
1 onion, sliced
2 carrots, diced
2 celery ribs, diced

1 x 14oz (400g) can chopped tomatoes
¼ bunch of parsley
1 bay leaf
2 sprigs of fresh thyme
1 tbsp flour
1 tbsp butter
⅔ cup dry sherry

1 Heat the oil in a large saucepan, season the oxtails with salt and pepper, add them to the hot oil, and cook until golden on all sides. Add the onion and cook until softened slightly. Add 2 quarts (2 liters) of water, season with salt and pepper, and simmer, uncovered, for about 2 hours. Cover and continue to simmer for another 2 hours. Check to see if you need more liquid during cooking, and add as needed.

2 Add the carrots, celery, and tomatoes. Tie the parsley, bay leaf, and thyme sprigs together with kitchen string and place in the pan. Bring to a boil and simmer for 30 minutes, or until the vegetables are tender.

3 Remove the herb bundle and discard. Scoop out the meat, remove from the bones, and discard the skin and bones. Strain the stock, reserving the vegetables. Refrigerate the stock for an hour or more. Using a blender, process the meat and vegetables and set aside.

4 Once the stock is chilled, remove the fat from the top and discard. Reheat the stock. In a large, dry frying pan, brown the flour over high heat. Cool slightly. Add the butter and blend. A little at a time, stir in the stock and the meat-vegetable purée. Season with salt and pepper to taste, and add the sherry just before serving.

A favorite from Goa in southern India, the vindaloo is Portuguese in heritage and notable for its garlicky masala, spiked with wine vinegar and softened with sugar.

pork vindaloo broth

SERVES 6   **PREP** 35 MINS PLUS OVERNIGHT CHILLING   **FREEZE** UP TO 3 MONTHS
COOK 3 HRS   AT THE END OF STEP 3

6 dried red chiles
1½lb (650g) boneless pork belly with rind,
   cut into 1 x 2in (2.5 x 5cm) chunks
1 tsp cumin seeds
½ tsp black peppercorns
6 garlic cloves, coarsely chopped
2 in (5cm) fresh ginger, coarsely chopped
1 tsp sweet paprika
3 tbsp tamarind pulp
3 tbsp white wine vinegar
4–6 tbsp vegetable oil

2in (5cm) cinnamon stick
2 star anise
3 onions, finely chopped
¾ cup white wine
1¾ quarts (1¾ liters) chicken stock
2–3 tsp palm sugar or dark brown
   (muscovado) sugar, to taste
salt
1 red chile, seeded and cut into
   strips, to serve
2 tbsp fresh cilantro, to serve

1 Soak the chiles in hot water for 10 minutes (for a milder flavor, remove the seeds first). Put the pork in a pan, cover with boiling water, bring to a boil and simmer for 5 minutes. Drain, discard the liquid, and set aside.

2 Dry-roast the cumin and peppercorns (see p25) and grind using a mortar and pestle. In a small food processor, process the ground spices, drained red chiles, garlic, ginger, paprika, tamarind, and vinegar. Set aside.

3 Heat the oil in a pan. When hot, cook the cinnamon and star anise for 30 seconds. Add the onions and cook for 10–15 minutes. Add the spice paste and cook for 1 minute. Pour in the wine and stock and bring to a boil. Add the pork, turn the heat down, and simmer for 2 hours. Chill overnight. The next day, scoop out the meat, strip away the rind, and dice. Skim the fat from the stock and strain the liquid into a clean pan.

4 Bring to a fast boil over high heat and cook for 5–10 minutes. Sweeten with sugar and season with salt. Before serving, stir in the pork and garnish with the chile strips and cilantro.

fruit

This is a soup that is easy to make in a hurry. All that's needed to bring out its fruity flavor is ample time to chill—and a perfectly ripe melon.

chilled melon and ginger soup

SERVES 4   **PREP** 15 MINS   **FREEZE** UP TO 1 MONTH
AT THE END OF STEP 3

1 ripe Galia melon peeled and seeded
1in (2.5cm) piece fresh ginger
1 tsp fennel seeds
7oz (200g) white seedless grapes
juice and grated zest of 1 lime
1 tsp dried mint
4 tbsp Greek yogurt, beaten
salt and freshly ground black pepper

for the garnish
2 tbsp fresh mint leaves
pinch of sugar
1oz (25g) crystallized ginger, finely chopped

1 Coarsely chop three quarters of the melon flesh into bite-sized chunks. Finely chop the remainder and set aside. Coarsely grate the ginger and squeeze any juice over the melon chunks. Discard the leftover ginger.

2 Heat a sturdy frying pan over low heat and lightly toast the fennel seeds for about 30 seconds, until you smell an anise-like aroma. Grind the seeds to a coarse powder using a mortar and pestle.

3 Put the ground fennel seeds into a blender with the chopped melon and ginger juice. Add the grapes, lime juice and zest, and dried mint. Process until smooth and push through a sieve to remove the skins.

4 Stir in the yogurt, season, and chill thoroughly—it's best to half-freeze this soup, then quickly whisk it just before serving. Spoon into bowls, adding a small pile of the reserved melon to each one. Shred the fresh mint with the sugar, mix with the crystallized ginger and scatter over the soup, then serve immediately.

Alfonso mangoes, renowned for their fragrant flesh and creamy texture, have a short season in India from early April through May. Other varieties work well too.

mango and curry leaf soup

SERVES 4   **PREP** 15 MINS **COOK** 20 MINS   **FREEZE** UP TO 1 MONTH
AT THE END OF STEP 3

for the garnish
small handful of curry leaves
vegetable oil for deep frying

for the soup
4 ripe mangoes, Alfonso if in season,
   available from South Asian stores
2 tbsp vegetable oil
1 tsp black mustard seeds
handful of fresh curry leaves

1 red chile, seeded, finely chopped
2 tsp palm sugar or dark brown
   (muscovado) sugar
½ tsp turmeric
2 tsp rice flour
1¼–1¾ cups vegetable stock
1¼ cup coconut milk
juice of 1 lime, to taste
salt and freshly ground black pepper
2 tbsp chopped fresh cilantro

1 First make the garnish: deep-fry the curry leaves in hot oil until crisp—it only takes a few seconds. Drain on paper towels and set aside.

2 Coarsely chop the flesh of 3 mangoes into small pieces and finely dice the fourth. Set aside. Heat the oil in a medium pan and, when hot, fry the mustard seeds for a few seconds before adding the curry leaves and chile. Continue frying for 30 seconds, until the leaves stop sputtering.

3 Add the 3 chopped mangoes to the pan, reserving the diced mango. Turn the heat to low and simmer the fruit until softened. Stir in the sugar and cook until the mango begins to caramelize. Sprinkle over the turmeric and rice flour and cook for 30 seconds, stirring all the time. Pour over 1¼ cups of the stock and simmer for 10 minutes.

4 Add the coconut milk and simmer for 2–3 minutes. Sharpen with lime juice, season with salt and pepper, and stir in the cilantro and diced mango. If the soup is too thick, add a little hot vegetable stock. Divide the soup between the bowls and sprinkle with a few crisp-fried curry leaves.

in praise of...
berries

In the summer, freshly picked berries are ideal for making wonderful chilled soups in a matter of minutes. All you need is a little sugar, lemon, and a smoothing touch of yogurt or cream.

cheese

breads

This basic white loaf is soft on the inside, with a light texture. If you have any left the day after you've baked it, use it for croûtons (see p39).

crusty white loaf

MAKES 1 LOAF **PREP** 35 MINS, PLUS RISING **COOK** 40 MINS **FREEZE** UP TO 6 MONTHS

3 cups bread flour
1½ tsp instant yeast
1¼ tsp salt

1 tsp sugar
1 tbsp vegetable or olive oil
1⅔ cups tepid water, as needed

1 Stir the flour, yeast, salt, and sugar together in a large bowl. Make a well in the center and pour in the oil. Stir in as much of the water as needed to make a soft dough

2 Knead on a lightly floured work surface about 8 minutes, until smooth and elastic. Shape into a ball. Turn into a large oiled bowl, and turn to coat. Cover with plastic wrap. Let stand in a warm place about 1 hour, or until doubled in volume.

3 Oil and flour the inside of a 9 x 5in (23 x 13cm) loaf pan, and tap out the excess flour. Punch down the dough. Shape it into a rough rectangle to fit the pan and place in the pan. Cover with plastic wrap and let stand about 30 minutes, or until almost doubled in volume.

4 Preheat the oven to 425°F (220°C). Dust the top of the loaf with flour. Cut a shallow slash down the center of the loaf. Bake for 20 minutes. Reduce the oven temperature to 400°F (200°C) and bake for 20 minutes more until the loaf sounds hollow when removed from the pan and tapped on the bottom. Transfer to a wire rack and let cool.

The mix of white and wholemeal flours in this loaf makes it lighter and moister. If the recipe seems complicated, it is actually much easier and quicker than it sounds.

wholemeal loaf

🍳 **MAKES** 1 LOAF 🕐 **PREP** 35 MINS, PLUS RISING **COOK** 40 MINS   ❄ **FREEZE** UP TO 6 MONTHS

1⅔ cups bread flour, plus more for kneading
1⅔ cups whole wheat flour, plus
  more to dust
1½ tsp instant (fast-rising) yeast
1 tsp salt

¾ cup hot water
¾ cup whole milk
1 tbsp vegetable oil, plus more for the bowl
1 tbsp honey
1 large egg, beaten, to glaze

1 Mix the bread flour, whole wheat flour, yeast, and salt in a large bowl. Make a well in the center. Stir the hot water, milk, oil, and honey together and pour into the well. Mix to form a slightly sticky dough. Cover with plastic wrap and let stand for 10 minutes.

2 Knead the dough on a lightly floured work surface for 8–10 minutes, or until it is smooth and elastic. (The dough will remain slightly tacky—do no add too much flour.) Shape into a ball, place in a large oiled bowl, and turn to coat with oil. Cover loosely with plastic wrap and let stand in a warm place for 1 hour, or until doubled in size.

3 Oil and flour a 9 x 5in (23 x 13cm) loaf pan, and tap out the excess flour. Briefly knead the dough on the work surface. Press the dough into a rough rectangle and place in the pan. Cover loosely with oiled plastic wrap. Let stand in a warm place about for 30 minutes, or until doubled in size.

4 Preheat the oven to 425°F (220°C). Brush the egg over the loaf to glaze it, and sprinkle with a little whole wheat flour. Slash a few diagonal slits in the top of the loaf. Bake for 20 minutes. Reduce the oven temperature to 400°F (200°C) and bake for 20 minutes, or until the loaf sounds hollow when tapped on the bottom. Let cool on a wire rack for 10 minutes. Invert and unmold onto the rack and cool completely.

acknowledgments

Dorling Kindersley would like to thank:
Editorial: Susannah Marriot, Diana Vowles,
Constance Novis, Lucy Bannell

Recipe testing: Anna Burges-Lumsden, Richard Harris,
Lisa Harrison, Rachel Wood

Consultant: Carolyn Humphries

Prop stylist: Sue Rowlands
Food stylist: Jane Lawrie, Annie Rigg
Art Director for Photoshoot: Nicky Collings

Index: Hilary Bird

Useful websites
American Food and Wine Festival **www.awff.org**

Blue Hill **www.bluehillfarm.com**

Chez Panisse **www.chezpanisse.com**

The Cookbook Store **www.cook-book.com**

The Culinary Institute of America **www.ciachef.edu**

Honeybrook Organic Farm **www.honeybrookorganicfarm.com**

Local Harvest **www.localharvest.org**

Merridee's Bread Basket **www.merridees.com**

Organic Consumers Association **www.organicconsumers.org**

The Soup Box **www.thesoupbox.com**

Worldwide Opportunities on Organic Farms **www.wwoofusa.org**

Picture credits